Ten Thousand Choices

TEN THOUSAND

Choices

MASTER YOUR Choices, Change YOUR LIFE.

Rachel Radwinsky, PhD

MCT Associates, LLC

Cover design by Julie Hopkins

First Printing: 2018
ISBN 9781983152733 (pbk)
Management Consulting and Training Associates, LLC
Frederick, Maryland
www.TenThousandChoices.com

To my parents Judy and Charles,
to my children Avery and Jared,
and to my husband Edward,
thank you for your support and patience.

To the memory of my grandmother Perlene
and my mother-in-law Janet,
the choices you made set in motion so many beautiful
things, thank you.

Contents

PREFACE

Feeling stuck. Whether it's your career, relationships, finances, or health; feeling like you can't get traction is frustrating. Many of us feel we're not living the lives we dreamed of when we were younger. We're not making the most of the time we have. We are so worried about what is going on right now we can't see the path ahead. Our true purpose has gotten lost in the shuffle. Our time and opportunities are flying by as we stand still and watch. This leaves us unhappy and confused, without direction and purpose. We suffer guilt and frustration, because we're not getting where we want to go and don't have a clear vision of where that is. We know we can do better. Take my coaching client Jess for example:

Jess is going through a rough patch in her career. She has spent the past twenty years in a corporate Human Resources job. Even though it has provided for her family well enough, it has often left her uninspired. Jess is a down-to-earth, people-oriented person who thrives on positive social interaction and is one of the most optimistic people I know. She likes to work with her hands, making things and being creative.

Her day-to-day work, however, doesn't match her interests or her personality. She works in an office environment where the bulk of her daily tasks are accomplished alone on a computer writing PowerPoint® slides and emails, or leading conference calls with people she will never see in person. Her boss is a micromanager. She prefers to avoid personal interaction and critiques Jess's work through emails. Jess gets to work before 7:00AM and rarely leaves before 6:00PM, answering emails any time of the day or night, but it never seems to be enough. She is the sole person reporting to this manager, having no peers or team members with which to collaborate or commiserate.

In Jess's case, she has spent so many years plugging away at her company's annual goals, making sure she hits them, she has lost track of *her* goals. What is important to *her*? What are *her* interests? She hasn't taken time to think about her *own* vision for the future. Because of this it's difficult for Jess to make any choices that will help her get unstuck in her career. I see many cases like this, and it concerns me how many people are feeling stuck and unhappy at what should be a stable, satisfying point in their careers.

Anna, another client, is confronting the same basic issue— feeling stuck. She is facing a choice many moms at some point encounter. What do I do with my life now that the kids are [fill in the blank—in Kindergarten, more independent, going to college, etc.]? She chose to leave the workforce when her children were babies. Anna worked for seven years being a great mom, but now feels she has to start over from scratch to have a career she can call her own. Her youngest started school in the past year, and after a few months of enjoying the quiet (which was heavenly I am sure), she is ready to get moving. But doing what? In her case, the job she had before was okay, but not particularly thrilling, so she has no desire to return to that company. The career itself was also "okay", but a lot of the jobs in her field require a long commute and longer hours than she wants to work given her kids' schedules. She is not even sure if a job is the right option because her husband is afraid it will put a strain on the family. What if something happened to him? She knows she needs something to make her time more meaningful now, while safeguarding the future for her family. She just doesn't know how to take that first step.

A related example is Joe. His mother had a stroke five years ago which left her disabled and suffering. Although he has a brother and sister nearby, he is the primary decision-maker and advocate for her. He has taken on more than his fair share of her financial and emotional responsibilities for her round-the-clock care. He loves his mother dearly, but even before the stroke, she was suffering from depression and anxiety, calling him ten or more times a day for help or comfort or venting. Now he visits her daily, but she still calls at the same rate, and gets upset when he won't talk for as long as she wants. After five years of this, he feels burned out. His health and marital relationship are suffering. He feels paralyzed by the situation and guilty for wanting it to change.

They are working hard and grinding through the day-to-day successfully, but Jess, Anna and Joe have lost track of the big picture. Because they lack a clear sense of their purpose and direction, they feel it is impossible to make any of the initial choices that would help them move forward.

In my work as a consultant, my job is to help businesses get unstuck. I conduct strategic planning sessions, lead process improvement initiatives, coach individuals, and teach project management and employee development workshops. These are all geared toward moving the businesses forward by getting both teams and individuals unstuck and turning things around when a team or employee is failing. I found myself giving my friends similar advice that I give my clients. Figure out your ultimate goal before you make any smaller decisions. Make a step-by-step plan for big changes in your life, defining what success looks like and how you will know when you get there.

The tools and processes I use to help business clients succeed can be directly applied to "real life" situations, such as my friends' career or family problems. I realized I was already using bits and pieces in my own life and had been for years. I create project plans for family vacations, draw up process maps and organizational charts for managing my photos, use the Japanese 5S organization system to clean my house, and conduct mid-year and year-end reviews of my personal "performance". I just do it so naturally that I hadn't noticed what an insufferable nerd I had become.

Besides being embarrassingly dorky, I am probably a little nosier about other people's business than I should be. I blame my psychology background. I think it is fun to sit in the airport and in the few seconds I have as a person walks by, to try to come up with their story, based only on what I see. I can guess some of the choices they made that day by looking at what they are wearing, what they are carrying, the look in their eyes, how they carry themselves, or how fast they are walking. It's worse with people I know. I lie awake at night trying to analyze my friends' personalities. Or if I have a conversation with a family member that didn't sit well, I will dissect the interaction in my head over and over for anything I might have missed that would help resolve the situation.

My psychology background has trained me to be a good observer of people and a good researcher. To help people live better lives, it is critical to understand why they make the choices they do and explore how they can make better ones. It is within our power to understand the psychology behind our choices and to use practical tools to plan and control our choices so that we can improve our lives.

WHAT THIS BOOK IS:

This book is intended for anyone looking for help getting unstuck. The methods in this book can be applied to anything-- getting things done, advancing your career, improving your situation, being more productive and balancing the competing forces in your life. I didn't write it only for professionals stuck between competing mid-life career choices, but I also didn't write it only for resolving personal or family issues. You have to take it all into account to make choices that create the life you want and to be the person you want to be.

This book is hopeful, but realistic. Living a life with intent and purpose is hard. Everyone has a different starting point. Creating a meaningful life is all about making the best choices with the hand we are dealt, whether we started with good cards or not. It takes effort and sacrifice; planning and discipline. It also takes the resilience to brush yourself off and try again when you make bad choices, or if your good choices just don't pan out. When you make a wrong turn, adjust your route and keep moving forward!

Recalculating.

-GPS

This book provides a practical framework for making better choices. Drinking more water, meditating, doing yoga, bullet journaling and exercising more are all great choices. You already know that. I am not going to tell you what choices to make, you are the only one who can decide. This book and your **Ten Thousand Choices Master Plan** will give you a structure to focus your priceless time and energy on the choices that are going to make a significant difference in your life and your future. You will learn how to *recognize critical choices when they present themselves*, using tools to analyze the choices according to your own values and determine whether they will help you achieve goals or take you off track. You are already full of good ideas and intentions, but great thoughts alone will not get you there. The purpose of this book is to get you very focused and specific about what you want to achieve in your life, and to create a solid plan to make it happen. The only thing that is truly going to make the difference between staying stuck or moving toward your dreams is you and your choices.

Those who have spent time in the corporate world will recognize some of these tools. Adapted and customized for "human" use, they are the same strategic planning, project management and accountability tools that companies use to evolve and grow. Throughout this book, I will present examples from my own life and from people I know. These are common everyday choices we all face, and some will sound quite familiar. Some are sad, some are funny, but all contain one thing—the never-ending opportunity to change and make different and better choices going forward.

WHAT THIS BOOK IS NOT:

The planning process and the tools and methods I recommend are all informed by solid research and successful implementation, but it will not be discussed in depth here. I kept this book laser-focused on getting your plan written. After completing the assignments, you will have a solid draft of your plan down on paper. If you want to take a deeper dive, you will find a few books, articles, podcasts and research recommendations in the appendix. I also use my blog to pontificate on related topics. You can check that out too.

This book is not about how marketing strategies influence our product choices or how branding seduces us into making certain decisions. In general, consumer choice theories don't have much to say about strategic life choices or personal planning. Where there is an intersection, I'll point it out, but without covering how to make everyday decisions about groceries, clothing or refrigerators or avoiding being hypnotized by colors and catchy jingles.

Finally, there are an overwhelming number of choices we make on a daily, even hourly, basis. We are overloaded with information. It causes stress and often wastes our time. This book takes a different approach to handling stress in the face of staggering "choice overload". Unlike a lot of the daily planners and organizers out there, the purpose of this program is *not* to organize your daily task list. That is simply going after the symptom, rather than the cause of the choice overload problem. Instead, it's about how to know when you're spending time on the important things, with a clear picture of the future you are working toward.

This is a framework for managing, controlling, prioritizing and evaluating choices. We are going to come at the problem of choice-overload from a different direction. You will define your guiding vision *first*, which you *must* do before you can make the right choices about how to spend your days.

Hundreds of little, everyday choices will still be there fighting for your attention. Going through this planning process will train you how to identify the important choices and ignore the noise and give you the direction to make the best decision in the situation. Your daily task list will get a lot easier when you know which things do, or don't, deserve your precious time.

How to Use this Book

Neither this planning process nor the Master Plan you create are ends in themselves. Rather, they are the starting point—the vehicle to drive your actions going forward. To get started though, you must have the inner motivation to work your way through this process.

You WILL NEED:

1.) A compelling reason for doing this program. Do you feel your life is not as meaningful or productive as it could be? At times it might even be spinning out of your control? Or maybe things are plodding right along smoothly? You are going about your daily routine without any major hiccups. The kids are growing up healthy, finances are stable, and relationships are solid. But gosh, it's already [insert month], and it seems like the year will be over before you know it. Then one year turns into the next, and it seems like you can't even recall one significant thing that happened, just that it was fast.

Now you're starting to look around and say to yourself, "Is this it?" That little whispering concern that you aren't doing all you could with the precious, short life you're given on this planet is starting to sound more like a primal scream. Yeah, me too. When I finally couldn't ignore the scream any more, I looked around for some solutions. This process is what works for me.

2.) The courage to prioritize *yourself* and your future happiness. It doesn't take a ton of time to do this, but it does take some concentrated *alone* time and effort to think through all your "stuff" and put your plan down on paper. Yes, I am talking about actually writing things down. On paper. With your hand holding a pencil. Or pen. Yes, it's a weird concept, I know. I cannot overemphasize the importance and power of writing things down. Until your thoughts are written down, they are ephemeral, momentary, changing, evolving and transparent. They are like the smell of honeysuckle on a summer breeze. A flash of light in the night sky. They catch your interest for a moment, but then are replaced by other thoughts, smells, sights, and they are gone. When you write your ideas on paper they become tangible. You can see them. You look away, and look back, and they're still there, free and available for you to analyze and dissect. As more thoughts fill in, you write those down as well, and eventually you have the whole story, the full picture of the situation for your use, now and later when you return to the paper with a new perspective, or different ideas. Take up the habit of writing down your ideas and thinking them through. Still not convinced? Research shows that writing notes by hand enables people to synthesize ideas, draw inferences and see connections better than typing notes on a computer.[1] So there.

If it isn't written down, it doesn't exist.

-Paul Gillard, PhD

So back to the *prioritize yourself* bit, this means putting your needs above everyone else's for a few hours. Find a way to escape, just for a little while, from the distractions and demands of everyone around you, and *think about you*. You deserve this. I'm not going to explain what alone time means—you know what I'm talking about. At times in my life, it has meant sneaking out to the garage and locking myself in my car for some beautiful silence (mostly when the kids were little—a version of hide and seek really). Or going to the library "just to return some books, be right back", and parking myself at a table for an hour (note to my husband—sorry about that). You probably don't even have to lie to your family to free up a few hours in a week.

Dang, just delete Facebook off your phone and there you go. No one in your family has to suffer, and you just freed up at least an hour a day. I'll leave it to you to figure out where the time is going to come from. We all have the same number of hours in the day. If you prioritize yourself, you will find the time. Plus, after going through this process you'll find that making a few targeted improvements in your life actually frees up *more* time in the long run. You can either take that new time and spend it on yourself or share it with the world. Your choice.

One of the things I realized is that if you do not take control over your time and your life, other people will gobble it up. If you don't prioritize yourself, you constantly start falling lower and lower on your list.

-Michelle Obama

3.) The discipline and determination to hold yourself accountable. This means envisioning your success and putting some clear measures in place to claim victory when you get there. Those measures will also provide warning signals that you may be falling short of where you want to be. Having that open mind to give yourself a little "tough love" feedback now and then can be hard, but healthy. The good news is that this program helps create a flexible plan to achieve your goals in spite of setbacks.

Following the three parts of this process, completing the assignments within each part, and finishing it off with your Master Plan is your first major move toward getting control over your choices. Going through this for the first time should take anywhere from a few hours to a month. It depends on how long you take to ponder your future, and how much alone time you are able to schedule at once.

HOW THE BOOK IS LAID OUT:
INTRODUCTION

This is the philosophical stuff where I explain how and why we make the choices we do, as well as some thoughts on life in general. It's not that long, and you may even want to come back and re-read this later.

Introduction	Part One: Look Back	Part Two: Look Around	Part Three: Look Ahead	Conclusion
The Power of Choice	Assignment 1: Personal Style	Assignment 3: Personal Summary	Assignment 6: Guiding Vision	Assignment 9: Accountability
	Assignment 2: Past Choices	Assignment 4: Core Elements	Assignment 7: Goals and Choices	
		Assignment 5: Priorities	Assignment 8: Master Plan	

PART ONE: LOOK BACK

Now we start with the practical stuff. The first step is to take a dive into your personal history, because like it or not, past behavior is often the best predictor of future behavior. To improve future choices, it's necessary to take a look at some of the choices you made in the past and fully understand your own decision-making preferences and habits. One assignment in this part will be to answer the question, "Where have I been?" by analyzing past choices and lessons learned.

Personal Style (an aspect of personality) can tell a lot about decision-making tendencies, as well as what you are likely to be thinking and doing immediately before and after a choice is made. We'll spend time exploring personal style with a short and easy assignment.

PART TWO: LOOK AROUND

The second part will focus on where you are today and what you're doing with your life right now. You will examine your current situation—your strengths, weaknesses and capabilities. This will be critical for making changes going forward, because choices must be made within the confines of your personal reality. The second assignment will be to determine the factors that are most important in your life, the things you value, love and cherish. These will provide the framework for how your future choices are made.

PART THREE: LOOK AHEAD

What would you like to be doing? Your first step in Part Three will be to define your personal guiding vision, the written statement of what you want your life to be. From there, you will set and prioritize goals for the things you value most in life, all perfectly aligned with your guiding vision. These goals become the choices that will make up the Master Plan.

CONCLUSION

The final part of this book discusses the what happens after the planning is complete. Execution of your Master Plan is essentially the *beginning* of your work toward your vision. Advice for getting started, staying motivated and *owning your choices* is provided.

This book provides written instruction to complete the planning process from beginning to end. There are nine assignments, and they work when best completed in order. Each assignment contains a few tasks broken down into a couple of straightforward steps. I describe each task in detail and give you some examples to help illustrate how to complete it. The examples are compilations of real people and actual situations, woven together to present an authentic view of the choices we all have made, are making, or will make at some point in our lives. My interviews with them were emotional and heart-rending at times, but also hopeful, inspirational and uplifting. I am so very appreciative of their openness and willingness to share their dreams and plans. You'll be able to use some of the ideas and lessons learned from their experiences in your own plan.

Upon completing the nine assignments, you will establish the foundation of your Ten Thousand Choices Master Plan. This document will contain your guiding vision, values, evolving priorities and detailed action plans that you create, execute and celebrate. You may choose to write your notes in the blank worksheets in the companion workbook or write on plain old white paper. After completing the assignments, you may find that maintaining your plan over time is easier with one the many project planning tools and apps available, including the old standby, Microsoft Excel®. However, until you get the hang of the thought process that drives this program, I strongly encourage you to start with pencil and paper. You will be able to use all of your brain power on the problem at hand, rather than half on the problem and half on how to use the technology properly.

INTRODUCTION: THE POWER OF CHOICE

It is our choices, Harry, that show what we truly are, far more than our abilities.

—Dumbledore, Harry Potter and the Chamber of Secrets

We make choices every day about our health, our relationships with our family and friends, our work, our finances, our physical space, our appearance, our communities, and more. These are the important choices. On top of that, we're constantly making choices as we shop, drive and interact with the world around us. Then in the background of all these conscious choices, there is the ever-present din of Facebook posts, political updates, world events, meetings, emails, phone calls ... the list goes on. Each one of these can present us with choices—whether to read it or not, whether to believe it or not, whether to act on it or not. The noise is deafening. It's overwhelming.

The next time you're at the grocery—one of the larger chains—count the number of Vlasic (or similar main brand) pickle types. Not the number of jars or the number of pickle brands in general, or even the number of sizes of Vlasic choices, but the number of types of pickles from one single brand of pickles. I ignored all the relishes and peppers and just focused on straight up pickle choices and stopped counting at twenty-five. I counted five in the Vlasic "Stackers" line alone—these are the big cucumbers that are sliced lengthwise to ensure they fit on no kind of sandwich I ever eat. Perhaps a foot-long sub, but who is building those things at home? Maybe Subway is putting Vlasic Stackers on their subs (I didn't research to find out), but I've never had a valid use for a Stacker. I don't think I have ever had a Stacker, unless I accidentally chose one of those jars over a jar of spears, clearly the better pickle shape. Side note: I think this is one of the reasons I like shopping at Costco so much—they only had two dill pickle choices the last time I looked, and I happily bought a gallon of spears just to be done with it.

Anyway, at least three minutes have passed while contemplating pickle choices. I'll make a flurry of other choices as I walk the aisles (don't get me started on the cereal aisle). Then I make some more as I drive home (CHOICE: honk at the jerk that breezed through the four-way stop, or just let it go), carry in the groceries (CHOICE: force my teenager to put down his phone and help me or just stew over no one helping me) and then put them away (CHOICE: ask who left the empty granola bar box in the pantry, or just toss it out and say nothing). While out and about, I may also have to make the choice of answering a text (CHOICE: buy Girl Scout cookies from a mom who knows I also have a kid in Scouts, or politely decline), responding to email (CHOICE: sign up to make a dessert for teacher appreciation week or ignore this third request with lots of capitalization and exclamation points), returning an overdue library book (CHOICE: do a U-turn and drive back to the library, or just pay another day's fines), seeing a woman I don't know very well (CHOICE: smile and say hi or turn away quickly so I don't make eye contact), and buying an iced coffee (no choice here, it's always a yes). If I'm lucky, when I get home I can zone out for a bit as I sip my coffee and be choice-free for a few minutes. But on average, I'm probably making some sort of conscious choice at least every three to five minutes during my day.

That is about twenty conscious choices every waking hour, or around 350 per day (assuming you get eight hours of sleep, if you are lucky). That is somewhere in the ballpark of 10,000 conscious choices per month. Give or take.

TEN THOUSAND CHOICES

If you're making around 10,000 choices per month anyway, what would happen if you made some better ones? What if just 10% of the 10,000 were better? The Ten Thousand Choices Master Plan will help you pick out the most critical choices that directly affect your vision for your future. It will help you recognize those choices and will be preloaded with the *right* choice. All you have to do is seize the opportunity.

No matter what you are personally working through right now, it is a fabulous time to be alive. You have so many choices presented to you that previous generations didn't. The world is quite literally at your fingertips. You can sit at your computer and find an answer to just about any question you can dream up. You can touch an icon on your phone and see where the people that are important to you are and what they are thinking about. And best of all, you can be reasonably comfortable that, due to advances in medical care and public safety, you will live to a ripe old age as will your friends and family. Heck, you even have at least five different types of Vlasic Stackers to choose from.

Most importantly though, if things go off the rails—if there are financial hardships, if a job ends, if someone gets sick, if some series of unfortunate events (a great book series by the way) unfolds—know that because of the wonderful time in which we live, and in this world of boundless opportunity (regardless of what the political pundits say), you are capable of identifying opportunities and making good choices. Everyone is. And even if things aren't going south, being able to make the good choice over and over, maybe even 10,000 times a month, will bring you closer and closer to your vision.

What is a Choice?

Every choice contains two conditions and one driver:

Choice = Selection + Volition + Want

CONDITION #1: There must be *selection*—the situation must present valid options from which to choose. For example, to make a choice about which school to send your children to, there must be different educational options to consider. To make a choice about how you are going to face a breast cancer diagnosis, you must have different treatment options to consider. To make a choice about how to repair your relationship with a friend, you must consider what conflict resolution options you have at your disposal. Without valid options, anything you do is merely an action, not a choice.

CONDITION #2: The second condition is *volition*. The decision must be yours to make using your own free will to do so. For example, work is often not within your control, so a lot of what you do on the job is not a choice. There are parallel choices you can make such as your attitude and effort and reactions, but often the work task itself is assigned by someone else. If that other person is making a choice that you are acting on, it might be *their* choice, but it isn't yours. Again, it is merely an action. Additionally, if someone else is forcing, requiring or otherwise compelling you to act, that's not a choice either. Finally, if you are not in a place emotionally, mentally or physically where you can freely choose, it's not a choice.

THE DRIVER: The driver of every choice you make is what you *want*. Assuming you have options and you have the free will to choose, your choices boil down to your judgement about what you want to do. Now before you say "Well, I do things all the time that I don't really want to do, like go grocery shopping or drive the carpool", or "There are lots of things I want to do, but I just don't have the time", let's be clear on the word "want". I didn't say "like", I didn't say "enjoy", and I didn't say anything about intentions or time. I said "want". And by that, I mean you take into account all the options you have and all the influencing factors surrounding the choice, then use your own free will to choose the option you judge to be best. By definition, that is the option you want. You may not *like* going to the grocery, but you *want* to have food in the house, so you choose to go. You may not *enjoy* driving the carpool, but you *want* your kids to get to school, so you choose to do it. You may say you will help a friend with a project, but you don't *want* to choose it over your other commitments, so you don't help. You may not *love* your job, but you *want* income, so you slap a smile on your face and go in every single day and do your best.

People do what they want to do.

You will do what you want. You will believe what you want. You will make time for what you want. You will be what you want.

- Should's don't matter: You know you should wear your seatbelt. You know you shouldn't be late for appointments. You know you shouldn't litter. You know you should eat healthy foods. *What you choose to do is based on what you want.*

- Other people's wants don't matter: You know your mother wants you to call more often. You know your spouse wants you to stop cursing so much. You know your kids wish you would play outside with them more often. *What you choose to do is based on what you want.*

- Intentions don't matter: You intend to lose ten pounds. You intend to stop texting while driving. You intend to make more friends. You intend to call your cousin on her birthday. *What you choose to do is based on what you want.*

- Time doesn't matter: You don't have time to volunteer. You don't have time to clean out your car. You don't have time to write a book. You don't have time to look for a job. *What you choose to make time for is based on what you want.*

SO, WE WANT TO MAKE BAD CHOICES?

Well, yes and no. It is true that you are doing the thing that you *want* to do at the moment that you are making the choice. If the choice is bad, then yes, in a sense you wanted to make a bad choice. It's more complicated than that though, because you have different levels of goals and motivations operating within you all the time. Sometimes they are in alignment, and sometimes they aren't. For example, if your high-level goal is "be healthy", some mid-level goals that support that might be "avoiding junk food", "exercising", "eating organic", etc. Your everyday choices should support those goals: Saying "no" when someone offers you a donut, getting out of bed 20 minutes earlier to work out, paying the extra dollar for the organic apples at the grocery, making the time to cook at home instead of eating fast food, and so on. But even though your high-level goal is "be healthy", you may still choose to eat the donut, even though it is not aligned with your goal and hence a bad choice. You chose it because at the moment you made the choice, you wanted it.

These smaller choices are the ones that matter. They are the ones that will move the needle. Your challenge is essentially to figure out what you want at the high level then change your minor, everyday wants be the ones that support and help you fulfil these important, life-changing goals. That is easier said than done though. There are many reasons people "do what they want to do" even though it's a bad choice. Most fall into the following categories:

- Acting out of habit
- Failing to recognize that a choice with other options exists
- Giving in to their worst impulses
- Doing nothing at all

As we go through each of these, try to think of some examples. These could be your own choices, or those of friends or family, or examples from well-known public figures.

ACTING OUT OF HABIT

Some of the most common "bad" choices are driven by habit, which make it so we act upon our wants automatically, without thinking. While some habits are good, many are not. Unfortunately, a lot of those bad habits are health-related. We settle into a pattern of eating crappy food, avoiding exercise, smoking, or any number of other self-destructive behaviors, ignoring the fact that every time we engage in these behaviors, we're making a choice. We all know that the most obvious way to lose weight is to exercise regularly and to eat healthy foods in appropriate amounts. Therefore, when confronted with the urge to eat when we are not hungry, our rational choice should be to *not eat.* Or maybe to grab a celery stick instead of a candy bar. Unfortunately, habit kicks in and blinds us to the choice in front of us, and we grab the ice cream container out of the freezer and polish it off before our conscious mind has a chance to enter the debate. Meanwhile, somewhere in our brains, there's a quiet voice saying, "Wait a minute, I thought we were trying to lose weight?". That voice, though, has no authority. It has not been given the freedom or the tools to challenge the habit, and so it's ignored, and the brain never even registered this as a choice. The same goes for all the other habits that we know are bad but choose to do anyway, such as sitting on our keisters instead of exercising, being chronically late, compulsively checking our phones, watching junk television, slouching, and overspending.

IGNORING OPTIONS

A variation on this is failing to recognize other options available. Again, out of habit, you walk to the kitchen when you're hungry. Besides the celery stick or the ice cream, do you consider the other options? If you slow down a bit and think about it, there are other conscious choices you can make. It could be making a U-turn at the fridge and going outside to get some fresh air. Another option might be to get a drink of water, because maybe you're just thirsty. Another option might be to go brush your teeth, because sometimes doing that will reset your brain to forget about eating for a while. When there is a choice to be made, but your perspective is so limited by your habits, or so narrow because you shut out options, you miss out on other (often better) possibilities.

GIVING IN TO THE DARK SIDE OF HUMAN BEHAVIOR

Every person has impulses and tendencies that when not properly managed, can cause bad choices. Later in this book you will spend some time thinking through your own impulses – those that are part of your healthy personality and those that may be getting in the way of your success. At the extremes, these unhealthy tendencies are similar to the ancient "Seven Deadly Sins" that have been around in some form or another for centuries. Here are some examples of how these negative impulses drive our wants and play out in our everyday decisions:

- *Sloth (Laziness):* This first "sin" is a broad one that most people are guilty of at some point or another. It is generally defined as "not doing things that should be done". The person is fully capable of doing the thing, but chooses not to due to indifference, apathy or lack of motivation. An underlying tendency to be lazy will lead to choosing the easiest or most convenient option, but often not the best option. This might be choosing TV over house repairs or choosing to nap over working on a resume.

- *Greed:* A person who tends to be greedy or selfish will make self-serving choices that ignore the needs of others or attempt to get more than they need or deserve. This typically applies to money and material possessions. People who fall for get-rich-quick schemes are making those bad choices based in part on greed. Sometimes greed makes people discount important information while making decisions—who wants to read the fine print on a too-good-to-be-true mortgage for your dream house (even though it is clearly out of your price range), or who wants to consider the instability of cybercurrency stocks when you think you have a hot stock tip that will make you millions (but for an investment you can't really afford)?

- *Wrath (Anger):* Rage, hatred and vengeance are hallmarks of this "deadly sin". Like all of these impulses, every person feels anger at times. It is how the impulse manifests itself in a person's decisions that matters. A person who flies off the handle easily will not only make rash choices but will drive away all the people who could help temper and guide her decisions. We all know someone goes into fits of screaming rage on the sidelines of their kid's sporting events every weekend. Or someone whose road rage has gotten so bad you fear for their safety. Or someone whose mood swings so quickly you feel like you are walking on eggshells when you are around them.

- *Lust:* Most people think of scandalous sexual desire when they think of lust, but this impulse can also be an unhealthy or compulsive desire for anything--money, power, control or material things. As far as deadly sins go, this isn't the worst of the lot, but everyday choices driven by lust, from flirting inappropriately to having extramarital affairs, can ruin relationships and damage reputations.

- *Gluttony:* We all overindulge at times, but the gluttony impulse takes overindulgence to an extreme. In terms of everyday bad choices, any form of overconsumption to the point of waste or selfishness can be gluttonous. So, eating too many cookies at the Bible study meeting is one thing, but eating all the cookies so that no one else gets any is gluttony. It is not limited to food either— taking more than you need of anything, especially to the point that other people get little or nothing is a bad choice to make.

- *Envy:* Similar to greed and lust, envy is the unhealthy desire for something someone else has. This propels the person toward choices that either strive toward getting whatever it is, so they feel equal to or better than the other person ("keeping up with the Joneses") or trying to take the thing away from the other person (or at least hoping they lose the prized item or status). An everyday example is a person who feels jealous that her neighbor got a new car, so she immediately goes out to get a newer and better model. Another example is a person who feels jealous that her coworker got a promotion, so she talks behind their back about how she only got it because she is friends with the boss outside of work. Additionally, this impulse can play out in the form of feeling joy or satisfaction from learning or witnessing the troubles or failures of someone that you envy. Interestingly, this phenomenon is common enough to have an official name—it is "schadenfreude"[2].

- *Arrogance (Being Selfish and Inconsiderate):* This is a biggie as far as the original framers of the seven deadly sins were concerned. Formerly called "pride", this impulse is thought to be the source of the other sins and is defined as "dangerously corrupt selfishness—putting your own needs and wants before the welfare of others", as well as being egotistic and condescending toward others. Examples of everyday choices driven by pride might be that person cutting line because *they* are in a hurry (like I'm not?) or have more important things to do than everyone else waiting in line. Or that braggy person everyone calls "Topper" behind her back because no matter what anyone is talking about, she will have a story to top it. People who put their own needs and feelings far above others are easily recognized. They are the controlling "know-it-alls" in your volunteer groups, the outspoken critics of everything and everyone on the community Facebook page, and the inconsiderate neighbors who flick cigarette butts on the sidewalk and don't pick up after their dogs.

One last impulse that must be called out combines a few of the sins listed above. It is *passive-aggressive behavior*. It contains the hostility of wrath, with a little bit of selfishness and envy sprinkled in and a shot of sloth for good measure. I call it out specifically because although it is common, it is sometimes difficult to identify its effect on choices. This tendency makes a person present themselves as compliant and willing, but all the while they are privately resentful, hostile and bitter about their choices.

Sometimes people choose this course of action on purpose—perhaps as a way to influence someone else's behavior, or as a way to provoke someone else to make the first move in a conflict. Other times, people choose passive-aggressive behavior because they are in a situation where they can't directly challenge or confront a person or problem, so they engage in unproductive behaviors to work around the issue.

Possible clues that someone is being passive-aggressive when you are working with them on a project or dealing with them in a day-to-day interaction are they use sarcasm when they disagree, instead of communicating directly. They become overly critical about minor decisions and details. They consistently choose to show up late or choose to leave early. They claim forgetfulness when they don't deliver on something. The clearest sign though, that someone is being passive-aggressive, is subjecting others to "the silent treatment". Can you think of anyone who voluntarily takes on huge tasks and turns away offers of help but then becomes bitter, sulky or blames others that they are overburdened and doing all the work themselves?

How about someone who is constantly late or always manages to make everyone else wait?

It is hard to keep these impulses in check, and it is normal to give in on occasion. When you see a life-long pattern of not being able to identify and manage these tendencies, you see these people repeat their mistakes. They plunge right in to the next pyramid scheme that comes along. They get right back into debt after completing the bankruptcy. They quit their next job in the same fit of rage. They volunteer for another project even though they are still silently fuming about the last one.

I have the choice of being constantly active and happy or introspectively passive and sad.

-Sylvia Plath

DOING NOTHING

The last and perhaps most frustrating reason for making poor choices is *doing nothing* when confronted with an important choice. Here's a career example: You've been struggling to get your crafting business off the ground. Over dinner, a friend says she could introduce you to someone who owns a boutique downtown that dedicates a portion of their floor space to local crafters. You excitedly say, "Yes, thank you" and promise to follow up with her on Monday. However, Monday rolls around and you are busy with kids and cleaning the house, and maybe you have a bit of a headache. You figure it will be okay to wait until Tuesday to call. Then a week goes by and you're embarrassed to call because it has been a whole week, and you said you would call on Monday.

At least three different choices presented themselves to you during this simple interaction. First, you could have chosen instead of, "I'll call you Monday" to make more definite plans to follow up with your friend, such as scheduling a meeting (and put it on the calendar right then and there). Or, if you had already made the choice weeks ago to get those business cards printed, you could have handed her one at dinner. Those two choices aside, the next would be to make it a priority to contact her on Monday. It seems daunting to call someone and ask for a favor—but she offered, and *it was yours for the taking.* Now you've been presented *three times* with the choice to get new business and you chose the wrong option! Finally, at the end of the week, you *still* have the choice to track down your friend's number, call her up and ask if the offer to make the introduction is still good. Granted, your delay has made it a little harder, but you still have the choice to act (or not). In this case the failure was *doing nothing.*

So, which of these are critical, life-changing choices? How would you know? If you don't have a clear idea of where you are going, you won't be able to tell important decisions from everyday noise. Changing this last example slightly, suppose you had a plan. You would know that one of your top priorities for the year is to build your crafting business. You would also know that one of your high priority goals to get you there is to make ten new connections with local companies. Given that this interaction presented you with a choice that would *directly* affect the achievement of a goal, this would qualify as a critical choice (more on building such a plan later).

If you don't know where you are going, any road
will get you there.
—Lewis Carroll

The common thread among these examples is that consistently making good choices is not a given. It takes effort. The challenge isn't in the choice itself, it is in how well you have prepared yourself for making the choice. This includes being aware of your natural tendencies and managing them accordingly and in planning for how you will handle the choices that come your way. This planning will increase the percent of your ten thousand choices that move you toward your guiding vision for your life. It starts with 1) establishing that vision and 2) having a plan to get there that identifies the choices and tells you ahead of time what choice should be made.

The Unbreakable Rules of Choice

RULE NUMBER ONE: YOU ARE THE PRODUCT OF YOUR CHOICES

You are the sum total of all the choices of your life up until this very moment. This might be a little dose of tough love— wherever you are at this exact point in time—you got yourself here. You and all your many choices. Big, little, good, bad. You, today, are the legacy of a lifetime of choices.

Big, little, good, bad. You today are the legacy of a lifetime of choices.

You may be saying, how about all the crappy things which happened that I didn't ask for? Was that a choice? It's absolutely true that horrible, devastating, unfair things happen. People are born into bad situations—abject poverty, violence, drugs, crime, and neglect. Bad things happen along the way. Moms get cancer. Friends die in car wrecks. People lose their jobs. Teenagers accidently become parents. Loved ones get addicted to drugs. Bad things happen even when you have all your ducks in a row and make all the best choices. No doubt about it. Bad things happen that you don't choose, *but your reaction to those things is entirely your choice.* You may in some cases have limited choices immediately around the event, but as time goes forward (as it always does), different paths will emerge and your choices about how you think, feel and behave will determine that event's impact on your life.

Life is ten percent what happens to you and ninety percent how you respond to it.

-Lou Holtz

Not doing anything is also a choice. In this program, we count everything, whether it's an action or an inaction, as a choice. Unfortunately, many of the inactions in our lives are simply another example of poor choices—ones that keep us from reaching our goals and ultimately our vision for the future.

When you choose to turn on the TV and spend the two free hours that you have in an evening watching sitcoms instead of working on your business plan, that is a choice. When you choose to read Facebook posts for an hour rather than sit and chat with your daughter about her day, that is a choice. When you choose to stay in your car at school pick-up instead of getting out on the blacktop and connecting with some other moms, yep, that is a choice.

Blaming someone or something else is a common reason behind inaction. People can be awful at times and situations can seem unfair but using that as an excuse not to act puts you in the position of being a victim. It takes away your power, and over time becomes an ugly habit. In addition to blaming people, we unfairly point our fingers at competing priorities or tiredness or forgetfulness or fear for our inability to deliver on the promises we make to ourselves.

Personal accountability is the only remedy for this disease of inaction. I'm going to be direct—don't be lazy, don't look to blame someone else, don't be passive, don't complain. Think through your issue, plan a little, and then do something to make it better. When you think about how you make your choices, you'll spend time sorting through all the barriers that keep you from succeeding, including motivation and prioritization, so that you have the tools in hand to select the best choice and act on it.

RULE NUMBER TWO: ALL OF YOUR CHOICES MATTER

Life is so very short. Life is short even when it isn't *cut short* by all the tragic things that can happen to moms and dads and kids and friends and colleagues. Let's face it, our productive years on this planet are limited, so the importance of each action feels amplified the older we get. Is every daily choice we make life-changing? Maybe not, but each one counts in some way toward who we are and who we become in the future.

Each choice counts in some way toward who we are and who we become in the future

---

When I was graduating from college and unsure what to do with my psychology undergraduate degree, my uncle said I should talk to his friend Mary because she did "something psychology-related". I'm shy, an introvert, and was even more so at the time. The last thing I wanted to do was call up some lady I'd never met and talk about- —what? I didn't even know. This hardly even appeared on my radar as a "choice", it was just a suggestion from my uncle, and one that could easily be ignored. But it *was* a choice and ended up being one that shaped my future. I weighed the options—either feel guilty because I didn't do what my uncle advised (guilt—I could write another whole book about that) or endure an awkward conversation with a stranger. Avoiding guilt won out, I called the lady and had a nice, painless conversation. I made my uncle happy, thus relieving my guilt, and I came out of the conversation with a nugget of information that would change my future.

Mary had gone to college and earned a degree in psychology, just as I had. Also, just as I had, she worked with the mentally ill for a while and realized that it just wasn't her calling. I had spent the previous summer volunteering at Western State Hospital in Hopkinsville, Kentucky. Nicest people in the world, dedicating their lives to do work that I knew was not a good career fit for me, and I had just spent four years working on a degree to do just that. Up until that summer, I had been working to check off all the to-dos to start the application process for graduate programs in Clinical Psychology. Now I was just sitting at home wondering what the heck to do next. Not Clinical Psychology, at least I knew that much.

That's where Mary came in. I made a choice that at the time didn't strike me as an important decision. It was, after all, just a courtesy call, but one that led me toward a different career path. Mary was an Industrial/Organizational Psychologist[3]. It seemed like all the fun, interesting aspects of psychology that sold me on it in college—helping people, figuring out what makes people tick, watching people in social interactions, and trying to predict people's behavior. I could still get a graduate degree, and I could still work in psychology, focusing on "people in organizations" rather than in a clinical setting.

Calling Mary wasn't a *huge* choice in and of itself, but it was pivotal. It suddenly and forever changed my path forward. It opened up new choices that I didn't, until that moment, realize existed.

One decision to do something (or not) can change your whole life.

RULE NUMBER THREE: YOU CAN MAKE BETTER CHOICES ANY TIME YOU WANT

To make a commitment to do something differently and—– Simply. Do. It. You don't like how you look? Make choices that will change how you look. You don't like how you feel? Make choices that will change how you feel. You aren't happy with your career? Make choices that will change your career. You aren't happy with your personal relationships? Yep. Make choices that will change your personal relationships. Change your choices, change your life.

Choices that align with clear goals, which in turn align with a guiding vision, are the key. Research studies have demonstrated time and again that setting goals does three extremely valuable things that many other motivational and self-improvement techniques fail to do[4]. First, setting goals has been proven to increase the amount of effort you put into a task. Second, it increases your persistence and likelihood of sticking with the task until it is

45

finished. Third, goal-setting provides the direction and guidance for your choices, quite literally pulling you toward your dreams.

You can't go back and change the beginning, but you can start where you are and change the ending.

-C.S. Lewis

Because I'm making a bold statement about human behavior, I'll balance it with a *caveat*. There are plenty of opinions in this world about how and why people end up in the various predicaments and troubles they experience. I agree that a great deal of the problems we have can be traced back to bad choices that we are 100% responsible for making. However, some people go as far as claiming that every single thing we do, think and feel are choices. In extreme cases, that even includes physical and mental illnesses[5]. I wouldn't go that far. I would also exclude situations where people don't have a reasonable amount of freedom or control over their situations, such as victims of abuse or those living through war or extreme poverty. Sometimes a person's starting point puts them at such a disadvantage that no amount of good choices can make up the deficit. This book is not meant to be an admonishment for them. For those with no such excuses though, we have a lot more power and control over our choices than we think (or acknowledge).

How We Make Choices

For decades, researchers and business experts and generally smart people have proposed many different perspectives and views on how humans make choices—also known as judgements, preferences, distinctions, determinations, alternatives and, last but not least, decisions. Many books and articles have been written on the process[6]. A commonly accepted model of how we make decisions usually goes something like this:

1. Determine the problem
2. List some possible solutions
3. Decide on the best solution
4. Implement the best solution
5. Assess the outcome

If you've ever gone through the process of buying a car, chances are you theoretically went through some version of this process. You determined that you needed a new car (problem). You probably thought of a few types of cars you wanted (list solutions). You picked one (best solution) and bought it (implement solution). As you drove it around, you were treated to a constant reminder of whether it was a good choice or not (assess outcome).

This captures the essence of decision-making at the point of the choice itself, but it leaves out much of the extra noise and mess that we have going on while enduring our daily barrage of choices. We humans are complex creatures, and the choices we make can be just as complex. Without even being aware of it, we process a whole host of psychological, social, economic and emotional factors when we make decisions. We not only have to consider the choice of A versus B, but we also take into account the situation, our past experience with A and B, other people's opinions of us for choosing A or B, the other options C and D that may be available in the future, and how A or B might fit (or not) with other choices we have made or will make. To make matters worse, multiple choices may be demanding our attention simultaneously.

Back to the car purchase. Beside the buying choice itself, there are all sorts of internal factors contributing to your choice. Was it a spur-of-the-moment decision, or one that was planned far in advance? What was your budget? How much time did you have to make the choice? Was the decision yours, or were there other opinions involved? What were your requirements for this car? Safe? Sporty? Good gas mileage? Dependable? Lots of options? Cheap? Had you ever purchased a car before, or was this your first time dealing with the car sales rigmarole that inexplicably takes a minimum of six hours even though most of the time you are sitting alone in a room? Are you good at negotiating, or does it make you break out in hives?

To complicate matters even more, the world presents us with constant challenges and curve balls that affect our choices. Back at the car lot, you may find that the car you wanted is not in stock. Or that your salesperson won't strike a deal you can live with. Or due to a computer glitch, you can't get your bank loan approved today, but could get that six-month same-as-cash car lot deal with all the fine print. Or someone else swoops in and scoops up your dream car before you can seal the deal.

When you think of all the factors that go into the choice, along with the actual decision you are trying to make, the process is more complex than the five-step process covers. I think these steps make sense for the actual decision to be made, but let's consider what else is contributing to the choice.

INTERNAL INFLUENCES

Of course, the choice happens inside your head, and is influenced by all the things going on in there. You have transient, short-term influences such as your mood and physical state (how awesome are your choices when you are hungry, sleepy or mad?). You also have enduring, longer-term factors like your personality, personal values and your skills and abilities that drive your decisions. In addition, you manage to factor in the roles, responsibilities, commitments, obligations and core elements that give your life meaning. Whether you are conscious of it or not, all of these things weigh in during your decision-making process.

These internal factors will be discussed in depth later. Controlling them is one of the key levers for improving the quality of your choices and the direction of your life. CHALLENGE: TO BE SELF-AWARE

EXTERNAL INFLUENCES

There are factors outside of your control that affect your conditions for making choices. Time, money, resources, schedule and other factors can set limits on what choices you make. In addition, the information you are given, whether accurate or not, has a huge influence on your decisions. Although you can't necessarily control some of these external forces, you can make plans to mitigate the issue or assimilate the factor into your choice.

CHALLENGE: To UNDERSTAND HOW ENVIRONMENT AND OTHER EXTERNAL INFLUENCES AFFECT CHOICES

OPPORTUNITIES

Choices present themselves all the time. Will you have the oatmeal or the donut? Will you go back to school or not? Will you speed up on the yellow light or slow down? Will you answer the phone or ignore it? In the assignments, we will spend a significant amount of time on goal-setting and planning. These activities will position you to be ready for opportunities—to recognize them when they occur and identify and consider all of your options.

CHALLENGE: To RECOGNIZE THE CHOICE EXISTS AND CONSIDER YOUR OPTIONS

STRATEGIES

Everyone uses some sort of decision process, what does yours typically look like? Do you use the basic five steps--think about the problem and select the best alternative based on the available information? Phone a friend? Flip a coin? Cross your fingers and hope for the best? Ignore it until the choice is made for you or the opportunity is gone?

The point is, you already have within you some strategies to make choices. There are lots of different ways to make choices, sometimes we use the thinking, reasoning portions of our brains, other times we react based on our emotions, sometimes we "go with the gut" and sometimes we rely on luck. During the course of the program, you will add *new* tools to your decision-making toolkit.

CHALLENGE: TO MAKE THE CHOICE THAT SUPPORTS YOUR GOALS AND VISION FOR THE FUTURE

ACTIONS

Your choice could be to do nothing. Or to procrastinate. Or to knock the ball out of the park. Whatever it is, this is the part of the process that depends on your ability to carry out the choice you have made. This program will provide you with some tools to kick-start your motivation or drum up the courage to make the choice that pushes you toward your vision.

CHALLENGE: TO OVERCOME INERTIA, BAD HABITS, PROCRASTINATION AND FEAR

OUTCOMES

Just as your car's GPS says "recalculating" after you make an unexpected turn, your life's path will readjust with each choice you make. If your choices happen to be part of the plan guiding you toward your vision, then there's not much to adjust. Just give yourself a pat on the back and continue to the next choice. Not all choices are perfect though, and if you have a good, solid plan in place and a clear vision guiding you, your mistakes will simply require a recalculation and an update of your plan.

CHALLENGE: TO BE RESILIENT IN THE FACE OF FAILURE, GRACIOUS IN THE FACE OF SUCCESS, AND NO MATTER WHAT, KEEP PUSHING FORWARD

OWNERSHIP

This program centers on you and the power you have to determine your future. You are influenced by internal and external forces that determine how you will receive the opportunities that life present you, process the choices and turn them into action. You are accountable for the decisions you make, for your reactions to situations, and for your choices to act in one way or another.

CHALLENGE: OWN YOUR CHOICES

LET'S WORK THROUGH SOME EXAMPLES

To sum up the process, you're confronted with a choice, then you're influenced by all the various internal and external forces swirling around, you pick a decision strategy, you make your decision, then you act on it and deal with the consequences. Think back to some of your past choices. What were some of the things about the situation or about your mindset at the time, that led to that choice? Do any of these examples sound familiar?

FRIENDSHIP CHOICE

In a group text with your girlfriends, someone responds to a text you sent with something that you interpret to be critical and snarky. You are confronted with a choice about how you respond. External influences are that you are in a hurry, trying to run an errand over lunch. You're already having a stressful day at work because your boss is being a jerk. The available information you have is this one snippy text, preceded by several days of radio silence from the whole group. You are already annoyed with them because they keep canceling plans at the last minute. Internal influences are that you feel very loyal to this group of friends, but lately feel like they aren't being considerate of your time and effort to keep the friendship going. You know you tend to be a bit of a stickler when it comes to being on time and making sure everyone is contributing equally. You are tired and feel like you are being treated unfairly, and frankly you're not in the mood for any attitude this afternoon. And you aren't the type of person to ignore a rude text.

So, with all that preloaded, you enter your decision-making process. The choice you have is how or whether to respond to the text. The options you consider are to return fire and zing her right back, or take a deep breath, put your phone back in your pocketbook and ignore the text. What other options might you have? If you act on that option, what might the outcome be for you and for your friends?

CAREER CHOICE

You've been feeling stuck and stagnated in your job for a while. You're uninspired and chronically exhausted by the long days and long commute. But the idea of going through the job search process sounds more daunting than dealing with the job.

One morning at 3:00AM, you wake up to the ding of a condescending, belittling email from your micromanaging manager. External influences are that there are 400 other things you have totally nailed this week, but she is demanding to know why you haven't scheduled a trivial meeting with three people who have already communicated to you both that they are out of the country this week. Internal influences are that you have the tendency to procrastinate, especially when there might be significant change or discomfort involved. But it's 3:00AM, you're wide awake now (and angry), you open up your resume on your computer. This is it. Finally, the impetus you needed to start your job search, and the first decision toward that is to update your resume.

Unfortunately, your email is also open and up pops a social media update, "So-and-so has tagged you in a photo!". It's a distraction that you know could derail your resolve to finally update your resume (another external influence combined with the internal influence of a raging Facebook addition). With those two things competing, you have a choice to make and see two options—work toward improving your career by updating your resume or kill an hour on Facebook and get even less sleep tonight. What other options should you consider? What would you do and what are the likely outcomes of your choice?

FINANCIAL CHOICE

You finally saved up enough to take the family on a nice vacation— finances have been tight, so this is the first in several years. The external influences are that you only get two weeks of vacation each year and you are using almost all of your days (as well as your savings) on this trip. A lot of your friends have visited this place, and you have seen their photos posted on social media. The internal influences are intense: A yearning to give your kids an awesome experience and make wonderful memories with your family, a need to take a much-deserved break from your stressful job, and a petty desire to one-up the Facebook crowd.

You splurged on a spectacular hotel with a view and using airline points you were able to get an upgrade to business class well. The splurging hasn't stopped with that though. You booked excursions for each day and bought specialized gear to go along with each excursion. You need to get new clothes for yourself and the kids, but the credit card just reached the maximum charge limit. You will be confronted with many financial choices before, during and after this trip. Each time you are presented with an opportunity that adds to the overall cost of the trip, you will consider options that either contribute to your family's fun or contribute to your debt or both. Given you have a financial limit that you have already reached, how will you prioritize your needs? What actions will you take and what are the expected outcomes in the short and long term?

These may seem like trivial choices. Certainly, these aren't the type of life-changing choices we often think of when tackling the issues of friendship and career. However, these are the everyday choices that incrementally drive our lives in one direction or the other.

How do we force ourselves to make the right decision? What if we had a guiding vision in place, influencing the internal side of our choice process? This vision might contain some thoughts along the lines of "nurture the relationships we value" or "have an inspiring and lucrative career" or "live debt-free". What if we also had some written goals containing ideas like "pause and think before reacting in tense situations" and "don't use text messages or Facebook to resolve conflicts" and "conduct job search targeting manager level jobs closer to home" or "set a vacation budget and stick with it".

Give yourself a fighting chance to make a good choice.

Simply having gone through the process of thinking up those goals and writing them down on paper will be enough to cause you to pause for a second, pick a good strategy for making the choice, then acting on it. That is all we are doing here— giving ourselves a fighting chance to make a good choice. We won't *always* make the right choice, but this will make it more likely. The more good choices we make now, the better positioned we will be to make them over and over in the future!

Takeaways:

- People are rational creatures who can think and make conscious choices.

- Choices require selection and volition, and assuming you have those two things, the choice boils down to *what you want.*

- There are three unbreakable rules for making choices:

    o You are the product of your choices.

    o All of your choices matter.

    o You can make better choices any time you want.

- Goal-setting will increase your likelihood of making better choices by motivating you to act and guiding your choices in the direction of your vision.

- Write down your thoughts and ideas—if it isn't written down, it doesn't exist.

PART ONE: LOOK BACK

Assignments:
1. Personal Style
2. Past Choices

Past behavior is often the best predictor of future behavior. To improve future choices, it's necessary to take a look at past choices and fully understand the impact of personal preferences and habits on decision-making.

Your Personal Style

Personality expresses itself through thoughts, feelings and patterns of behavior. It guides many aspects of a person's life, for example the types of people they are attracted to, the work they like to do, what they find funny, what they do in their free time and how they make decisions. Although moods and opinions can vary over time, even over the course of a day, throughout our *lives* our personalities and personal preferences stay fairly stable[7].

Personality is made up of a collection of characteristics or "traits" such as confidence, creativity, tact, and perfectionism. For example, if one of your stronger personality traits is "conscientiousness", chances are you act in a way that reflects your sense of self-discipline and responsibility. You complete things that you start, you are good at organizing, and people respect your ability to get things done. You might also avoid risks, feel uncomfortable with unplanned activities and sometimes resist change.

Knowing about these characteristics in yourself (and others) is useful—it makes it easier to make choices about your career (think Accountant versus Sales Rep), your hobbies (think home organization versus sky-diving), activities you might want to be involved in (and avoid) and how you want to spend your time. It also makes you more aware of your weaknesses and challenges. Consider these examples:

- A person with a strong conscientious personality trait may get stressed by changes and surprises and may not deal well with people who don't follow the rules. They may be perceived as rigid (maybe even stubborn) and may be a little controlling when it comes to working with others on projects or activities.

- A person who has a strong extroverted personality trait may have trouble working independently and get bored or demotivated with tasks that require more thought than action. They may be seen as less focused and more dependent on others to make decisions or get things done.

Looking back to the model of how people make choices, notice that personality (I will also refer to it as "personal style" or "personal preference"—for our purposes, it's all the same thing) is an important *internal influence* over your choices. Remember, the challenge you must overcome for the Internal Influences is to be self-aware. You must understand and appreciate how your personality style affects what you think and do. When you master that, you can start to use it to your advantage (for example choosing a career that complements your personal style), and you can use it to avoid putting yourself in no-win situations (for example a career that you struggle to enjoy and ultimately fail at because it just doesn't fit with your personality).

There are loads of personality theories and models and assessments out there, many of them excellent resources for increasing self-awareness. If you aren't familiar with this research and want to know more, then definitely check out some of the personality references I provide in the Recommended Reading section at the end of this book.

This is not a book about personality theories though, so we're going to take a short cut to self-awareness by adopting a super-simple personal style model that works well for our needs. It takes a high-level whack at personality type and doesn't drill down into the granular facets of personality differences. So, if you think of this tool as a surgical instrument, it's more like a hacksaw than a scalpel. If you have ever taken the Myers-Brigg's Type Indicator (MBTI) or one of the plethora of

Red/Green/Blue/Yellow personality typing tools out there, it's similar to those[8].

Another note about this personality assessment is that it is self-determining, meaning there are no tricks or hidden meanings in the sections and no forced-choice questions. It's not a test at all, it's a self-guided exploration to think through and determine your style. You'll learn about the four styles as you go through the exercise and select the one that best fits how you see yourself.

It's important to keep in mind that these personal styles are equivalent, and there is no best "type". Each has its own strengths and weaknesses when it comes to making good choices. In addition, we can have feelings and display behaviors that align with any or all of these styles, depending on the situation. The key is to understand what the predominant personality characteristics driving your decisions are and use them to your advantage. We'll do a little soul-searching to see if we can zero in on your personal style.

ASSIGNMENT 1: IDENTIFY YOUR PERSONAL STYLE

There are two steps in this exercise. First, you'll complete the short assessment to identify your personal style. Second you will explore your profile to gain a better understanding of how it affects your choices.

STEP 1: COMPLETE THE PERSONAL STYLE QUIZ

This begins with a brainstorming session about yourself—who you are and what makes you tick. Often people are surprised by how little thought they give themselves and don't realize it until they take the time to ponder these questions. To complete the assessment, read the questions then jot down your answers on a piece of paper. Write the *first words* that come to your mind and try not to overthink your answers.

Who are you as a person?

What are some words that describe who you are as a person? What are some words that other people might use to describe you? Where are your energies focused? What do you stand for?

What irritates you?

What are some things that upset you or make you unhappy? Write down the first things that come to mind when you think of pet peeves, annoyances and aggravators.

What do you enjoy and value in life?

What are some things that make you happy or that you enjoy doing? What are your favorite past times, interests, hobbies or activities? What is it about these things that make them enjoyable?

How do you approach decisions?

How do you typically approach a decision that you need to make? Write some short phrases that describe your usual approach, for example "I Google it" or "I ask my friends for advice".

Now that you've warmed up your brain a little, read through the words and phrases in the following sections, and circle any of the words you see in the columns similar to the ideas you wrote, or are additional words you might use to describe yourself. Circle as many words as you want from any of the columns.

**Try to limit your selections to the ones that you <u>feel most certain</u> about. Any of these could apply to most people at some time or another but try to select the ones that are the <u>most applicable to you, most of the time</u>.

Who are you as a person?

A	B	C	D
•Instinctual	•Cooperative	•Logical	•Responsible
•Laid back	•Easy going	•Thinker	•Loyal
•Bold	•Tactful	•Curious	•Task-oriented
•Spontaneous	•Sensitive	•Strategic	•Organized
•Open-minded	•Compassionate	•Independent	•Punctual
•Risk-taking	•Romantic	•Problem-solver	•Has high standards
•Free spirit	•Trustworthy	•Conceptual	•Respectful
•Adaptable	•Patient	•Philosophical	•Traditional

What irritates you?

A	B	C	D
•Boring routines	•Conflict	•Incompetence	•Wasting time
•Waiting in lines	•Rudeness	•Taking orders from others	•Chit chat
•Lack of freedom	•Feeling rushed	•Low standards	•Indecisiveness
•Rules and regulations	•Controversy	•Poor quality	•Not being prepared
•Apathy	•Being too competitive	•Overly emotional people	•Slow pace
•Stubborn people	•Aggressive people	•Making mistakes	•Being late
•Too many details	•Dishonesty	•Stupidity	•Irresponsible people
•Strict schedules	•Insensitivity	•Being embarrassed in public	•Confusion/chaos

What do you enjoy and/or value in life?

A	B	C	D
•Adventure •Friendly competition •Meeting new people/ socializing •Physical activity •Having fun •Excitement and stimulation	•Helping others •Showing compassion and kindheartedness •Being authentic and genuine •Team efforts •Reading about people and relationships •Being with friends and family	•Learning •Collecting things •Doing things efficiently •Reading about technical or scientific topics •New gadgets/ apps/ inventions •Figuring out how things work	•Getting stuff done •Doing good deeds •Organizing things •Leading activities/ coaching/ teaching •Tidying/ decluttering •Safety and security

How do you typically approach important decisions?

A	B	C	D
•Go by gut feel •Try not to overthink it •Keep options open •Use intuition over facts •Negotiate •Consider immediate benefits	•Gather opinions •Take others' feelings into consideration •Get the whole story first •Mull it over until comfortable •Reach consensus •Consider future possibilities	•Collect data •Think it through completely •Research the issues •Ask questions •Use reasoning and logic •Consider current situation	•Make a list of the options •Organize the facts •Plan it out •Consider customs and tradition •Be realistic and sensible •Consider past experiences

Do you see a pattern in your responses? The four personal styles we're interested in are represented by the four columns A, B, C and D in each of the sections. You may have noticed that most of your circles are in one or two of these columns. If so, your personal style is starting to emerge.

Go back through each section and count the total number of circled items you have in column A, column B, column C and column D. Add them up until you have a total for each column. Write your grand totals in the boxes below.

A's	B's	C's	D's

YOUR PERSONAL STYLE IS:

- If you answered mostly A's, your style is "Instinct". You don't need many details to make a decision, you instead focus on the big picture and tend to make quick decisions and don't look back. **Read your profile entitled "Instinct".**

- If you answered mostly B's above, your personal style is "Cooperation". You value relationships, and your interactions with others is a key part of your decision-making process. **Read your profile entitled "Cooperation".**

- If you answered mostly C's, your personal style is centered on "Logic". You look to data, facts and analysis before making a decision and enjoy solving a complex problem. **Read your profile entitled "Logic".**

- If you answered mostly D's, your personal style is "Responsibility". You tend to be cautious in making important decisions and approach them in a disciplined and organized manner. **Read your profile entitled "Responsibility".**

- If you answered with a mix of all styles (i.e., got a similar number for two or more types), then you may have a more flexible approach to decision-making, and aspects of your personality may offset or counter other aspects. Or which one you use may be dependent on the decision or the situation at hand. Either way, the similar scores may suggest that your style is more balanced, and no one style dominates. This is not a good or bad thing, it is just the way you are. To gain a better understanding of how the styles are working in conjunction with each other, read the profiles for your top two highest scores and think about how you *are* and *are not* like the profiles of those two types. Because it's difficult to differentiate your style, you'll need to pay extra attention to your internal thought process as you make decisions to be aware of how your personality is influencing you. You may also wish to ask others who know you well which of the four profiles they think best describes you.

FINAL QUESTION

In addition to better understanding your combination of these four personal preferences, you should also know where you are on the Introvert/Extrovert continuum. If you haven't heard of this before, here is a quick overview.

Introversion and extroversion are not simply measures of being shy or being talkative. This facet of personality says something about where we get our energy. An introvert will tend to "recharge their batteries" by looking inward and reflecting. When they spend time in large groups or around other people for a long period of time, they feel like they lose energy, and the way to get back to normal is to be alone with their thoughts. Directly opposite of that is an extrovert, who tends to re-energize by being with other people and doing outwardly-focused activities. Spending time alone or doing independent work *uses up* their energy, and they get it back by socializing with others.

There is no such thing as a pure introvert or extrovert. Such a person would be in the lunatic asylum.

-Carl Jung

As with all personality dimensions, extremely dominant traits are rare. We all carry aspects of each type into various situations, and our behaviors change accordingly. Anyone who identifies as an introvert can socialize and enjoy parties and make of fool of herself in front of a group, just like an extrovert. And anyone who identifies as an extrovert can enjoy a night alone at home, given the right circumstance. We exist on a continuum of traits, and in many cases may exist in the middle. Sorry for going a little academic on you, but even back in the 1920s Carl Jung (that famous psychologist) identified a large chunk of people that regularly sit right in the middle[9]. The name "Ambivert" has been given to this group somewhere along the line—meaning they display both introverted and extroverted tendencies equally. Like being ambidextrous with your hands. Only with your personality. Get it? Anyway, you can use this if the introvert/extrovert labels don't feel quite right.

Why is this important to know right now? Because so many of the choices that we make concern other people. We need to take into account our tendency to either welcome that interaction or avoid it. The differences between the two ends of the spectrum also say something about our communication patterns, impulses, deliberation and risk-taking—all important factors in decision-making. Understanding where you are on the continuum will help you not only with your choices, but in getting along with others in general.

So, with that in mind, answer the following:

Circle your place on each continuum below, then choose your overall preference

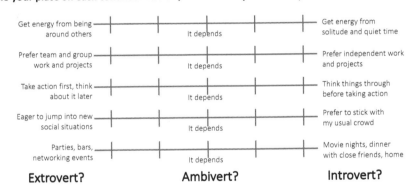

Decide where you are on the overall continuum for each pair of statements. Do you lean more toward the Extrovert or Introvert side? Or are you in the middle? Based on your answer, place and "e", an "i", or an "a" in front of your personality style (e.g., iResponsibility, eLogic, aInstinct, etc.). There you go. Read the profiles in the next section to see if yours is a good fit.

Remember that your dominant type is fairly stable and won't shift or vary depending on your situation or your mood, unless you consciously choose to behave differently.

MY PERSONAL STYLE IS: _____

STEP 2: EXPLORE YOUR PERSONAL STYLE PROFILE

Each of the personal styles are described below, with extra emphasis on how the characteristics of each style influence choices. Read through your profile descriptions first and decide if it feels like a good fit, or if another style or combination of styles fits you better. The decision-making tendencies will be important later in the program as you start setting goals and making plans for executing them. After learning about your own style, familiarize yourself with the other styles. In addition to managing your own tendencies, you can anticipate how other people are likely to make decisions and better manage your interactions with them.

INSTINCT

People whose dominant personal style is **Instinct** are highly creative, "out of the box" thinkers who can always be counted on to come up with new ideas and think on their feet. They tend to be quick-witted, good communicators, smooth networkers and highly sociable. At the extreme, they can come across as self-focused, irresponsible, impatient or untrustworthy. Their ability to influence others is a key strength, as are their energy, adaptability, and playfulness. They are adventurers, free-spirits, and risk-takers. Some possible careers for Instinct types are sales manager, real estate agent, party planner, lobbyist, or marketer.

WHAT THIS MEANS FOR MAKING CHOICES

The most notable thing about the way Instinct types make decisions is that they don't need many details—they focus on the big picture and make quick decisions. Instinct types are true to their names when it comes to decisions—they are instinctive! They can trouble-shoot issues very quickly and take action before others realize there is a problem.

Another key thing to know about their decision process is that unlike Logic and Responsibility types in particular, they don't typically fear making mistakes. They welcome change and take failures and setbacks in stride. This also means they seldom look back or waste time regretting past choices. Unfortunately, they may not learn from their mistakes and can miss chances to apologize or make amends for when they hurt others with their choices.

They get bored easily, thrive on stimulation, and like to make things happen. This leads to choices that on the positive side can be adventurous and fun, but on the negative side, chaotic and risky. More than any other type, they usually suffer from FOMO (fear of missing out), which sways their choices. They don't want to sit around and discuss things, they don't want to plan, and they don't want anyone to slow them down. Their choices can hurt the feelings of Cooperation types and frustrate the heck out of Logic and Responsibility types because of the lack of thought and structure they need to make a decision.

They tend to live in the "here and now", so their choices have a short-term focus. This can be admirable, as they embrace life and live it to the fullest every day. However, on the flip side, they don't always take the future into account and can make choices that are short-sighted and create problems in the long term.

DECISION CHALLENGES TO CONQUER

- Impulsiveness

- Difficulty in predicting or ignoring how current choices will affect their futures

- Impatience with others who want to talk about plans or think things through

- Changing their mind suddenly and going in a different direction without considering consequences

EINSTINCT: EXTROVERTED INSTINCT

Many Instinct types come across as extroverted simply because they are always on the go and in the center of activity. Most often that means they're with other people—recruiting others to participate in activities, negotiating and convincing others to do something, and often doing several things at once. Very often, they do fall on the E side of the spectrum.

IINSTINCT: INTROVERTED INSTINCT

Due to the very nature of the Instinct type, it can be difficult to spot an iInstinct—but they are out there. They may still spend time in the center of activity, but at the end of the day, they'll seek out alone time to recharge. You might also find them participating in adventurous, stimulating or fun activities (e.g., concerts, rock climbing, video games) alone.

ADVICE FOR THE CARE AND FEEDING OF AN INSTINCT TYPE

- Instinct types are not likely to plan or think things through carefully—help them by posing questions and providing high-level structure to guide them in the right direction.

- Try not to overwhelm them with details. Give them only the most important, high-level information they need to move forward.

- Take advantage of their ability to lead others through chaotic or difficult situations. They are amazingly good at ignoring the noise and getting to the cause of a problem and solving it.

- Give them feedback. They will not take it personally and will welcome it, even if it is critical.

- Stand back and appreciate them for the fun, entertaining, energetic and spontaneous people they are.

- Do not: Force them to adhere to a strict schedule or structure or make them spend any more time on detail and planning *than is necessary.*

- If your type is Logic or Responsibility, be extra careful that your attention to details and structure doesn't turn off an Instinct type and try not to get too irritated with them when they behave unpredictably.

COOPERATION

People with a dominant style of **Cooperation** are at their core relationship builders. They tend to be warm, nurturing, expressive and sensitive. At the extreme, they come across as too tender-hearted and perhaps naïve. Communication is one of their key strengths, as well as their ability to mentor, support and inspire others to improve their lives. Typical career paths involve using their people skills and compassion for others (e.g., nurse, social worker, teacher, motivational speaker).

WHAT THIS MEANS FOR MAKING CHOICES

The first thing to note about Cooperation types is that many (or most) of their decisions are made based on feelings—both their own and other's. They don't always have (or use) facts or data to support their choices, they tend to act on intuition. This isn't a bad thing, they are very good at reading other people, so are accurate about decisions that pertain to emotional responses and touchy-feely situations.

They are uncomfortable with conflict though and will avoid decisions that produce conflict. In some situations, this is a strength. They evaluate the emotional scene quickly and make choices that create harmony and peace. Because they're seen as fair and kind, other types tend to accept their decisions more easily. However, in cases where disagreement is unavoidable, they shut down, withdraw, waffle back and forth between options, or make a choice that eases the tension but doesn't solve the problem.

They find it more difficult than the other types to say no, so may make choices that help other people, but makes their own lives more difficult. Along this same line, they can become overly involved with helping others, sometimes to the detriment of both parties.

Cooperation peeps tend to take things personally, so it is important that they not let that sensitivity cause undue stress or overreact to imaginary insults. *If you are a Cooperation type and you took that last sentence personally, then you are reading the right profile.* They wear their hearts on their sleeves, and in many ways that is awesome — people come to them for a sympathetic ear, for a shoulder to cry on. They are the ones we seek out when we have a crappy day. They will cry with us, they will laugh with us, and we cherish them for it. They must, however, keep in mind that the sensitivity that we love them for can also cause them to make decisions that are not best for them in the long term.

DECISION CHALLENGES TO CONQUER
- Procrastination when the decision is likely to involve conflict
- Tendency to acquiesce (say yes), even though they shouldn't
- Being wishy-washy or waffling between choices
- Avoiding confronting issues head on when there is conflict or disagreement involved

ECOOPERATION: EXTROVERTED COOPERATION
Conversation is one of the favorite pastimes of Extroverted Cooperation types. Any sort of social outing is welcome, and the focus of the conversation will be on personal topics—relationships, recent interactions with others, and above all, feelings. Choices are made during these interactions—Cooperation types, especially E's, do not stew over choices on their own. They make the choice as they are talking with others—be aware of this!

ICOOPERATION: INTROVERTED COOPERATION

Behind the scenes helping, volunteering and caring for others is the joy of the Introverted Cooperation type. They love to talk about feelings and relationships as well, but in quiet, one-on-one settings. They too will make their choices during conversations with others, rather than alone with the facts.

ADVICE FOR THE CARE AND FEEDING OF A COOPERATION TYPE

- Physical touch is okay, welcome even.

- Allow them to express their feelings and try to open up about your own.

- Listen attentively and let them know they are being heard.

- Do not: Discount their feelings, be rude or blunt, ignore them, expect them to respond to conflict or disagreement.

- If your type is Logic or Responsibility, be extra careful that your attention to data and efficiency doesn't turn off a Cooperation type.

LOGIC

People whose dominant personal style is **Logic** are typically competent, independent and knowledgeable (about a little bit of everything). They are known as problem-solvers, thinkers and analyzers. They are less emotionally aware than other types and are sometimes seen as aloof or even arrogant. Their ability to process information and come up with the best solution to a problem is one of their key strengths, as is their insatiable curiosity and desire to learn. Typical careers for Logic types are scientist, college professor, inventor, or writer.

WHAT THIS MEANS FOR MAKING CHOICES

First and foremost, in order to make a decision, a Logic needs both data and time to think and reason their way through the issue. When the thinking process is complete, the Logic type will have strong convictions and stand by their choices. They are not wishy-washy and not easily intimidated. On the positive side, they are usually right about their choices. On the negative side, their decisions (and the blunt way they present them) may not take emotions or other people's feelings into consideration. This isn't always a bad thing, as many tough decisions fail to make everyone happy. A little finessing and acknowledging feelings could go a long way toward making their choices more accepted though.

Logic types tend to be overly concerned with appearing incompetent or "looking stupid" in front of others. Because of this, they withhold their opinions or delay making choices until they are 100% sure—which may be too late.

Logic types are surprisingly good at reading people, as they are observant and pick up and process cues from their environments easily. What makes them different from the Cooperation type though, is that they use what they learn from reading people simply as additional data, it typically doesn't sway them emotionally.

Communicating their choices and convincing others to rally around them can be a challenge. Because they are so confident in their decisions, they are sometimes viewed as a know-it-all or heartless. Remember, they have thought about the issue way more than anyone else, so they have a response to just about any argument that is presented. They just need to understand that their direct, and in some cases, brutally honest opinions do not always help their case.

DECISION CHALLENGES TO CONQUER
- Hesitance to share their own feelings and acknowledge the feelings of others
- Fear of making mistakes or saying things that make them look incompetent—this will make them delay choices or be overly conservative in their choices
- Need for excessive amounts of information and thinking time to make decisions—they may make choices too late to act
- Absolute intolerance of irrational or illogical behaviors and decisions in others

ELOGIC: EXTROVERTED LOGIC
Logic types are less likely to be strongly extroverted, as the nature of Logic is to be independent and deep thinkers—most of which has to occur when alone. Certainly, there are plenty of eLogic types out there, but their need for connection with others is usually based on a common interest or specific purpose (think club or association meetings rather than meeting for casual lunch or coffee). They often play "devil's advocate" in discussions and will sometimes walk others through their thought process by "thinking out loud". All Logic types are fairly cautious about jeopardizing their reputations by being wrong, so if they say something out loud, it is usually accurate.

iLogic: Introverted Logic

Many Logic types fall on the introverted end of the spectrum, again due to the nature of the type. That doesn't mean they are shy or afraid of people, they just don't feel the need to bring others into their rich internal worlds of ideas and thoughts. The iLogic types will rarely "think out loud" or express their opinions in large groups. They're also more comfortable keeping their feelings to themselves and will only open up to the people closest to them.

Advice for the Care and Feeding of a Logic Type

- Allow them to be self-sufficient, independent and free to make their own choices.

- Don't Google it, ask a Logic type! They love to share their ideas and what they know.

- Do not push them to respond or make a decision before they have had a chance to think—alone.

- Encourage them to smile more and give them a safe place to express their feelings and make mistakes.

- Do not: Discount their knowledge, be inflexible or limit their options to solve a problem, force them to use an illogical process, rush their decisions, or make them look stupid.

- If your type is Cooperation, be careful not to force your expectations about feelings and expressiveness onto a Logic type.

Responsibility

People whose dominant personal style is **Responsibility** are organized and efficient in most areas of their lives. They tend to be structured, cautious, traditional and have a strong sense of duty and honor. At the extreme, they come across as inflexible or controlling. Their ability to get things done is one of their key strengths, as is their ability to lead others and provide structure and common sense to any situation. Some example careers for Instinct types are accountant, Human Resources manager, home organizer, financial planner, judge, auditor and air traffic controller.

WHAT THIS MEANS FOR MAKING CHOICES

The most important thing to note about the way a Responsibility type makes decisions is that they will make the decision in advance and it will be carefully planned. They rarely put things off until the last minute and tend to get annoyed with people who procrastinate. They love to plan and make lists and timelines. They are goal-oriented—they set goals and have a clear sense of how tasks connect to larger actions that lead to achievement of those goals. Their choices will follow a linear path from start to finish, and they diligently work to see their decisions through to the end.

Responsibility types have a strong sense of what is "right" and "wrong" and what is appropriate behavior in a given situation. This tends to make their choices black and white, and they're uncomfortable with situations where they must choose a "gray area". They also get frustrated with people (particularly Instinct types) who are more comfortable bending the rules and/or violating social norms. Cooperation types may get their feelings hurt a little by the Responsibility type's decision process, because much like the Logic types, emotions take a back seat.

They follow rules, policies and procedures carefully. Their choices will almost always be based on a guiding rule—either an external law or policy or one that they hold as part of their strong internal moral compass. This makes it easier to make decisions, since the guideline is already there, pointing them in the right direction. This tendency keeps them safe and secure but may also keep them from exploring all their options.

This type also tends to make decisions based on tradition or status quo. They will sometimes go in a direction simply because that is the way it has always been done, rather than trying a new thing that could fail. They fear failure more than the other types, and because of this, their decisions are less likely to be risky or dangerous.

On the positive side, these tendencies make their choices steady and realistic, and keep their lives safe and consistent. They can make decisions quickly because their internal guidance is strong, and they follow it closely. On the negative side, they miss opportunities in life because there is often change or risk involved in new things or uncharted paths. It also makes change slow and difficult for them, and they may not change until forced to do so.

DECISION CHALLENGES TO CONQUER
- Tendency to deal in "absolutes" —things are either right or wrong, with no in between, and they may stubbornly dig in their heels on their choices

- Judgement of others who do not view the world the same way—they may tend to criticize or shame others for making choices they do not agree with

- Rigid adherence to lists, schedules, timelines and plans—this can limit their ability to adapt when things don't go as planned

- Tendency to micromanage or make choices for other people when they are stressed

eRESPONSIBILITY: EXTROVERTED RESPONSIBILITY

Responsibility types are fairly balanced along the E and I continuum. The E types are natural leaders who bring people together to discuss plans, assign tasks, give instructions and follow up to make sure everyone is marching in the same direction. They have strong verbal communication skills and will pick up the phone to address issues or discuss plans instead of emailing or texting.

iRESPONSIBILITY: INTROVERTED RESPONSIBILITY

This type needs time alone to plan and reflect. The organizing, planning and directing that iResponsibility types thrive on is typically done by way of spreadsheets, project plans and checklists, rather talking through the plans with others. They prefer electronic communications to track progress and communicate rather than in-person discussions.

ADVICE FOR THE CARE AND FEEDING OF A RESPONSIBILITY TYPE

- Acknowledge their hard work and dedication—it is often through their organization, efficiency and diligence that things get done.

- Show respect for their views on the world—you may not value a rule or policy, but understand they do.

- Encourage them to try new things, start new traditions and take breaks to have fun.

- Do not: Waste their time, insult their traditions, make them late, ignore their contributions, leave behind a mess.

- If your type is Instinct, be considerate of this type's need for structure and order. Bending rules and not following schedules causes them stress and frustration.

Your Past Choices

A good predictor of future behavior is past behavior, especially when we're thinking about choices we make over the short term and within the same environment. In other words, all things being equal, you will probably make similar choices over and over unless something changes. So, before you can harness the power of your choices to change your life, you first need to *understand the choices you have made in the past*—and what choices you're likely to keep making if you continue on the current path.

That is not to say you should obsess about past mistakes, especially to the point of derailing your future. The point is to learn from the past and understand that after a choice is made, it becomes an internal influence for future choices—*the experiences in the past affect your choices going forward.* After you learn as much as you can from these past choices, especially the mistakes, you must forgive yourself, clear your mind and move forward.

ASSIGNMENT 2: UNDERSTAND YOUR PAST CHOICES

There are three steps in this exercise. First, you'll brainstorm a list of past choices and think about the quality and significance of the choices. Second, you will select some of the notable choices of your life—both big and small, good and bad, that made you who you are today. Finally, you will analyze a couple of the choices to better understand your own choice patterns.

Step 1: Think about your past

Close your eyes and think of some of the life choices you have made. They may concern your job—your career path, what your daily work is like, where you work, and who you are working with. Other choices may concern where you live— where you are physically located, what type of housing situation you have, who you live with, or what your house looks like. How much money you have, what you drive, who you spend your time with, who you love, who you try to stay away from, and an almost infinite number of other outcomes are due to the choices you have made.

Organize those past choices a bit to get a handle on them. There are different types of choices—so to keep it simple, sort by the *size of the choice* and the *outcome*.

SHORT-TERM VERSUS LONG-TERM

All choices alter your path in some way. Imagine your small, seemingly trivial choices in terms of the "butterfly effect". It refers to the idea that small actions today can result in enormous effects in the future. The phenomenon shows up quite a bit in different areas of scientific research (everything from weather patterns to throwing dice) and is based on the theory that something as minor as a butterfly flapping its wings in Colorado Springs could create a ripple effect in the atmosphere and cause a tornado in Tulsa the next week[10]. Whether this is true or not, it's safe to say that you never know which of your small choices are going to snowball into something big and life-changing.

Here are some examples of smaller, shorter-term choices. These are the routine choices that get us through our days, weeks and months. These typically come and go without much fanfare. We may not always think of them as "choices" and usually act on them automatically. It is the cumulative effect over time that can be significant. Often these mundane choices have hidden, life-altering aspects that we can only identify in hindsight.

- Green tea with no sugar for my afternoon pick-me-up, or grande caramel macchiato?

- Go to the gym today, or just take it easy?

- The $200 jeans, or the $20 jeans?

- Get out of the car and talk to the other moms at pickup, or just sit here and look at Pinterest?

- Ignore the fourth call today from my lonely cousin, or pick up the phone?

- Put the bags of donation items in the trunk, or let them sit in the hall for another month?

- Follow through on the promise to ride bikes with my daughter this afternoon, or hope she forgets about it?

- Others?

Here are some examples of bigger, longer-term choices. We tend to pay more attention to these choices—these are sometimes the only ones that register in our brains as a "choice". They typically unfold over time and can be the culmination of a number of smaller decisions.

- Career paths and job choices

- Beginnings and endings of relationships

- Family decisions (such as getting married, having kids or moving)
- Large financial decisions (such as home or car purchases, vacations and retirement savings)
- Others?

YOUR TURN

Remember, past behavior is one of the best predictors of future behavior. If you're going to get a handle on your choices going forward, you must try to understand what has been driving your choices up until now. Answer the following questions about choices you made in the past and think about them carefully. As with all exercises in this book, jot down your notes on blank paper or use the forms in the back of the book—either way, *write your answers down*. Not only will it help you think, you will need them for later assignments.

SMALL OR SHORT-TERM CHOICES

These are routine decisions, some of which will have an impact over time, others may go unnoticed. Take a moment to think through some of your everyday choices.

What are some of the choices you have made so far today?

Think of your interactions over the past few days—what choices have you made concerning your close friends and family? Co-workers? Strangers?

What are some choices you have made regarding things you have purchased, eaten, watched, read, etc.?

What are some of your habits that you are aware of—good and bad?

LARGE OR LONG-TERM CHOICES

These are significant decisions that by themselves have changed your life. Take a moment to think through some of the single choices that had a significant impact.

What are some of your biggest decisions in the past year? In the past five years?

What decisions had a lasting impact on your life?

What are some significant choices regarding your family, finances, health and career?

Think of some of the major turning points in your life. What decisions led to them?

POSITIVE VERSUS NEGATIVE

Can you think of any choices that were miraculous strokes of genius? How about minor embarrassments and major disasters? Often the quality of a choice is complicated to determine —there can be good things that come from bad decisions and vice versa. You know when you're purchasing lottery tickets that you're probably wasting your money (bad choice). Hence the joke that the lottery is "a tax on people who can't do math". However, that one-in-a-billion winning ticket would look like a pretty smart choice after the fact.

So, with the benefit of hindsight, evaluate some of your past choices as having either a positive or negative impact on your life. You can continue to think about some of the choices you listed above or think of some new ones. We're going to select the most interesting of these to do a deep analysis.

POSITIVE CHOICES

These are choices that support you in achieving your goals and lead you toward your guiding vision. Think through some of the best decisions you made in your life.

What are you most proud of?

What do you consider your greatest accomplishments of the last year? The last five years? Of your life?

What are some things that you get the most compliments about?

What are some of the things you do on a daily/weekly basis that have a positive impact on your life?

NEGATIVE CHOICES

These are the decisions that prevent/inhibit you from achieving your goals and lead you away from our guiding vision. What are some of the negative choices you have made?

What are your biggest regrets?

What are some things from your past that you would change if you could?

What are some bad habits and tendencies you need to change?

What are some of the things you do on a daily/weekly basis that have a negative impact on your life?

STEP 2: IDENTIFY NOTABLE CHOICES

Look back at your list of choices and identify the key ones that brought you to where you are today. If you were to put a selection of these choices into your own personal "Hall of Fame", which ones would you choose? Give it a try. From your brainstormed list of past choices, pick the ones that had the biggest influence on where you are today. Draw the Notable Choices Worksheet (see example below) on a blank sheet of paper and place your choices in one of the quadrants based on their [relative] size and on whether they pushed your life in a positive or negative direction.

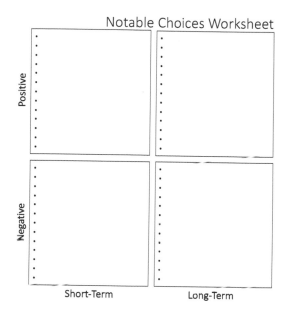

Notable Choices Worksheet

Each of the four boxes corresponds to Short-term or Long-term (the two vertical columns) and Positive or Negative (the two horizontal rows). So, the Short-term/Positive choices are on the top left, we can call those our "Tiny Triumphs". The Long-Term/Positive choices are top right, let's give ourselves some credit and refer to those as our "Stunning Successes". Those Short-term/Negative choices are bottom left, we can view those as simply "Minor Missteps" we made along the way. Finally, the bottom right contains the Long-term/Negative choices, and let's be honest and call those out as our "Massive Mistakes".

A QUICK ASIDE

As you go through this process, I'll throw a lot of things at you that you need to ponder, write down and think through. I know it can be a little overwhelming to learn a new tool or method *and* at the same time try to actually use it. I always found it helpful to see some detailed examples of how something is supposed to look when finished and work my way back from there. As you go through each step of the process, you will see each activity presented with a completed example. Then, when you're ready to complete your own, you can either write it up on a blank sheet of paper or get the companion workbook for the full set of instructions and worksheets.

One of the examples I use throughout is Cassie. As I mentioned earlier, Cassie's example is a compilation of several women's stories and experiences that may feel familiar. Her examples are real, and you may or may not agree with the decisions she made. Every situation is different, and none of us have the lock on perfect choices.

Cassie is a 45-year-old mom of two kids—a girl in middle school and a boy in high school. She is a jack-(jill?)-of-all-trades—she has a teaching degree and taught middle school for a while. But after her husband got a job transfer and they moved to a different state, she decided to try out a different career track (or two). She has jumped around since then—education blogger, tutor, Etsy crafter, substitute teacher. Now that her kids are older, she would like to focus more on her career and perhaps start her own business designing supplemental study programs.

She is sensitive and quiet and spends a lot of her time with her own thoughts. She tends to avoid social situations and because of this has had trouble meeting new people and making friends. She knows this is a problem area and wants to work on it but is not sure how. Her personal style is "iLogic" and she considers herself an extreme introvert.

When she turned forty-five she realized that (if she's lucky), she is at the midpoint of her life. If she lives to be ninety, she has about forty-five years left to do whatever else it is that she is meant to do. Considering how quickly the first forty-five went by, it doesn't seem like that long. Figuring out how to make the most of that time is important to her.

Okay, back to the "Notable Choices" assignment. Here is a completed example from Cassie to help you get started. In the Good—Big decisions for example, she put in her choice to not have three children. She and her husband debated whether or not to have a third child, and it was a decision they questioned for a while. Could they afford it? Would they have to get a bigger house? Did they really want to start over with diapers now that they were out of that phase with their youngest? For most people, this would qualify as a "big" choice. Now (in that rearview mirror!) she knows it was a good decision, so it goes in the Positive and Long-Term box, along with some good career decisions that she feels kept her on a job track that she liked. Likewise, she listed some choices that had a long-term negative impact such as a bad real estate investment that set the family back financially, and some regrets about not spending time with loved-ones before they died.

The short-term choices are more recent things that Cassie felt made an impact on her life. These will change over time, but the patterns of behavior will probably be consistent. Being involved in social and community activities are some of the shorter term positive choices Cassie has made. She highlights some known bad habits (sugar and anger management) and some one-time events (overzealous decluttering) in the negative short-term box.

Notable Choices Worksheet

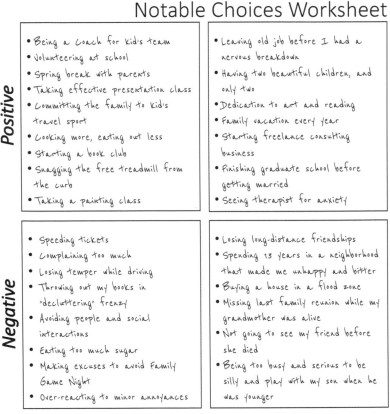

	Short-Term	Long-Term
Positive	• Being a coach for kid's team • Volunteering at school • Spring break with parents • Taking effective presentation class • Committing the family to kid's travel sport • Cooking more, eating out less • Starting a book club • Snagging the free treadmill from the curb • Taking a painting class	• Leaving old job before I had a nervous breakdown • Having two beautiful children, and only two • Dedication to art and reading • Family vacation every year • Starting freelance consulting business • Finishing graduate school before getting married • Seeing therapist for anxiety
Negative	• Speeding tickets • Complaining too much • Losing temper while driving • Throwing out my books in "decluttering" frenzy • Avoiding people and social interactions • Eating too much sugar • Making excuses to avoid Family Game Night • Over-reacting to minor annoyances	• Losing long-distance friendships • Spending 13 years in a neighborhood that made me unhappy and bitter • Buying a house in a flood zone • Missing last family reunion while my grandmother was alive • Not going to see my friend before she died • Being too busy and serious to be silly and play with my son when he was younger

Revisit this process yearly, and it's often a surprise to see that some of your choices change categories over time or others will drop off the list entirely. For example, Cassie made the choice a few years ago to stop complaining about her in-laws to her husband. This showed up on her Master Plan a few years ago, and it was a difficult habit to change, but she did well with it. Granted, sometimes she had to literally bite her tongue to stop herself, but it was hurting her relationship with her husband and she wanted to change it. When she revisited her plan this year though, she realized that negative choice didn't belong here anymore. The overall relationship with her in-laws had changed because of other relationship goals she put in place, and calling out her complaining was not relevant now, so she removed it.

Another thing you may notice over time is that some things you felt strongly about in the past aren't really standing out in your mind anymore. Perhaps you have made some new mistakes that are overshadowing the ones on the list, or maybe time simply caused the feelings to fade. Some however seem to be stronger than ever. You may get a little punch in the gut when you think of missed opportunities with loved ones who are gone. Even though it hurts to see it, it's critical to keep it front and center so that you don't squander similar choices you have the fortune to make with the people who are still here.

Our greatest glory is not in never failing, but in rising every time we fall.
—Confucius

Now it's your turn. Don't get caught up in the rules on how to use these tools. What is most important is that they end up being meaningful for you. If you need to refine what big/little or bad/good mean for you, have at it. The goal here is to identify the choices that you believe have made a significant impact on your life. I put them in this format to make it easy for you to refer to them as you go through this process, and they will become a permanent part of your Ten Thousand Choices book.

STEP 3: REFLECT ON LESSONS LEARNED

For this final step, think about the sum total of your past choices and decision-making tendencies. Document the overall lessons you have learned from your experiences on the Lessons Learned Worksheet (see Cassie's example) or on a blank sheet of paper.

Start by how you think about your choices. Do you typically notice when you're making an important choice? Do you have a method or steps that you consciously use when making a choice? This might be a Pros Versus Cons checklist-type thing that you write down. Or you usually call your significant other, parent or close friend to discuss a tough choice. Or you need alone time to think and make a decision on your own. Describe your typical decision-making process that captures the essence of how you typically make choices.

Your Choices in General

How do you typically make important choices?

Do you have a particular method or steps that you use to decide?

Second, think about which types of decisions are easier for you to make versus which ones have been more difficult. Easy decisions might be ones that you were able to decide more quickly, didn't require as much effort or thought, or that you didn't second-guess. Do these easier choices fall into any particular category? For example, you may find it is easier to make financial or career decisions than family or relationship decisions (or vice versa). Describe the types of decisions that come easier and perhaps you've had more success with.

Easy Choices

What types of choices do you find easiest to make?

What makes them easier for you?

On the other hand, think about choices that have given you the most trouble in the past. These are the ones hardest to make, taking more time and thought, or causing you to second-guess or waffle. What was it about those choices that made them difficult? Do they have something in common? Spend some time thinking through some of those choices to understand what it was that caused you grief. Describe them in detail.

> **Difficult Choices**
>
> What types of choices do you find to be most difficult?
>
>
> What makes them such a challenge?

Next, across all of your choices, what are some of the important internal or external influences that consistently affect your decisions? These might be things in your environment, your financial situation, home situation, other people in your life, your mental state, your personality or any number of other factors. What are some central themes you can identify?

> **Influences**
>
> What are some internal factors that consistently affect your decisions?
>
>
> What are the external factors that often influence your choices?

Next, think about what you would do differently. Particularly for the "bad" choices, what could you have done to prevent some of those mistakes? What would you do now, if you could have a do-over?

Do-Overs

What would you like to change about the way you make choices?

What would change if you had a do-over on some of your choices?

Finally, think back to the personal style questions we discussed earlier. What are some aspects of your personal style that typically dominate your choices? Have any of the choices you listed been inconsistent or contrary to your personal style? Describe these in detail.

How Your Personal Style Affects Your Choices

What are some aspects of your personal style that really come out when you make choices?

Have any of your critical choices been inconsistent with your personal style?

To summarize your Lessons Learned, fill in the blanks with what you learned about yourself and your past choices in *Part One: Looking Back.*

In general, I think my past choices have been:

Looking back on my past choices, I now realize that I:

My personality influences my choices by making me more likely to:

I think I could make my choices better in the future by:

Cassie's Lessons Learned Worksheet is provided as an example.

Lessons Learned Worksheet

Your Choices in General • How do you typically make important choices? • Do you have a particular method or steps that you use to decide?	I do a lot of internet research and make "pro versus con" lists. I also look for advice from my husband and close friends. I probably over-analyze things and wait too long to make decisions.
Easy Choices • What types of choices do you find easiest to make? • What makes them easier for you?	Decisions about kid and family activities are easy. The kids are old enough now that they can take an active part in choosing what they want to do, I am the gate-keeper to ensure that the schedule is manageable and we don't overbook or overspend. I think this is easy for me because I like managing projects and timelines.
Difficult Choices • What types of choices do you find to be most difficult? • What makes them such a challenge?	Financial and career choices are hard. The well-being of the family and our future is riding on making the right choices. I think there is too much worry and potential for guilt and regret built into a lot of the these choices, no matter what your decision.
Influences • What are some internal factors that consistently affect your decisions? • What are the external factors that often influence your choices?	Internal factors: Education, I feel my career choices are locked into the degree I have and even if I wanted to try something else I would feel guilty for not using my degree. Also my fear and anxiety get in the way of making different financial choices. External factors: Time and money, never enough of either.
Do-Overs • What would you like to change about the way you make choices? • What would change if you had a do-over on some of your choices?	I wish I could be more definitive and confident in my choices. I sometimes waffle and change my mind, and even after a choice is made I may try to go back and change it. Then I worry about it being the right choice. I would go back and spend more time with my grandmother before she died and have more fun with my kids when they were little.
How Your Personal Style Affects Your Choices • What are some aspects of your personal style that really come out when you make choices? • Have any of your critical choices been inconsistent with your personal style?	As an iLogic, doing research and thinking before making a choice fits with my style. Because of this I take a long time to make decisions and overthink things. I am not adventurous, but sometimes will choose the wild and crazy choice just because it is the opposite of what I usually do. But then feel guilty and embarrassed if it doesn't work out.

In general, I think my past choices have been	Well thought out, most of the time anyway
Looking back on my past choices, I now realize that I	Need to be more confident and stop second-guessing myself
My personality influences my choices by making me more likely to	Think it through carefully
I think I could make my choices better in the future by	Stop getting so hung up in the what-ifs and worries

So, what do we do with all the past choices? Refer back to RULE #1 — you can't change past choices—you have to accept what you have chosen in the past. You might say, "Hey, I could go back to school and change that choice I made about my career!". Yes, you can, but that would be making a new choice, and certainly one that can correct a decision that, in hindsight, was a bad one. However, this does nothing to change the old choice—it is still here, still affecting you today, and nothing you can do will change the past.

All is not lost though! *You can learn from your choices and choose to behave differently going forward.* That's the beauty of the situation and the most important point in this book—you have power over your choices. In the case of bad past choices, you can reduce some of the harm of the past, or at least fix some of the problems they created by planning and executing actions that change your course. Likewise, with a little planning you can make it more likely that you will repeat some of your good choices, and thus keep traveling on the path you want.

Change your thoughts and you change the world.
-Norman Vincent Peale

We'll spend the rest of this book deciding what exactly it is that you want and making a plan to get it. You have to accept though, that this is your choice. And will happen not because of one or two big choices, but because you make the right choice ten thousand times between now and then. You need to plan it out and be prepared for when those choices present themselves. What are you going to choose? Will you recognize the choice when you see it? Will you make the choice that takes you on the path to your goal?

PART ONE TAKEAWAYS:
- Personality influences many aspects of our lives, including how we make decisions.

- Assessing your own personality and that of others is a valuable tool for understanding choices.

- Past behavior is a good predictor of future behavior.

- Getting a handle on why you have made your choices in the past will begin your steps toward making better choices in the future.

PART TWO: LOOK AROUND

CHAPTER FOCUS:

Internal Influences | External Influences | Opportunities

ASSIGNMENTS:

3. Personal Summary

4. Core Elements

5. Priorities

Before you can start working on solutions, plans and actions, it is important to look around and get a clear understanding of your current reality. Think back to the choice model in the introduction. Internal and external influences are a key part of the decision process. If you remember, there were two challenges that these influences present: To understand how environment and other external influences affect choices, and to be self-aware.

Your Current Situation

The assignments in this section will help you overcome those challenges by helping you to become much more aware of what shapes your choices, both inside and outside of your control.

ASSIGNMENT 3: WRITE YOUR PERSONAL SUMMARY

This assignment will prompt you to think about your current situation. That is, where you are at this moment in time in terms of your unique circumstances. This includes both the *Internal Influences* that you have control over such as your skills and capabilities and the *External Influences* that you have less or even no control over such as available resources, the constraints and limitations in your life, and your overall environment. There are five parts you will complete for your Personal Summary Worksheet. We will go through each of the parts separately.

PERSONAL BIO

In this first section, answer the questions to create your Personal Bio. Imagine you are writing a resume, not for a job, but for your life, and this is the summary paragraph that introduces who you are and what is your story. It's sums up what you think of yourself and your current situation in just few sentences.

Who are you? What are the primary roles, responsibilities and commitments in your life? How do you describe yourself to others? What are your most pressing issues and concerns right now?

STRENGTHS AND ASSETS

These are all the good things you bring to the table. These are internal factors that you have the power to change. These are your skills, abilities and talents, knowledge you have gained, beneficial aspects of your personality, resources you have access to and in general anything that you can use to your advantage. Here are some examples:

- YOUR MAD SKILLS —Can you draw? Create awesome PowerPoint presentations? Solve problems? Enjoy giving speeches? Teach others? Are you good at a sport or physical activity? Maybe you are adept at a particular computer program or system? Expert at a craft or trade? Do you have any degrees, professional certifications or memberships?

- YOUR CHARMING PERSONALITY—Think about how you answered the personality quiz in Part One. Are you good at influencing people? Comforting people? Confronting people? Nurturing, caring for and helping people? Or do you prefer to avoid people altogether? Are you self-motivated? Organized? Conscientious?

- YOUR TALENTS—What unique things can you do? Are you a musician or artist? Good public speaker? Can you make people laugh? Are you a good writer? Can you tell a good story? Are you good with children? Animals? Are you a natural whiz at math or science? Good driver? Athletic?

- YOUR RESOURCES—What do you possess or have access to that can be useful to achieve your goals? A big basement? A big yard? A nearby library or community center with free space? A vehicle? Money available? Time you are willing to dedicate? Physical strength? A computer or other technology tools? Connections with other people who can help you?

What are your strengths and assets?

WEAKNESSES AND GAPS

Conversely, weaknesses are all the liabilities and disadvantages that we are aware of within ourselves, and that we have the ability to change. These might be skill and ability areas where education or development is needed, personality characteristics or impulses that block success, limited resources such as time, money or material items, and anything else that creates a disadvantage. Some ideas for your weaknesses may simply be a lack of some of the strengths listed above (i.e., you do not currently have the time, skill, or resources to do something you want to do).

What are your weaknesses and gaps?

OPPORTUNITIES AND RESOURCES

While you have at least some control over your personal strengths and weaknesses, opportunities and threats are external factors you cannot necessarily control, but that have an effect on your decisions. Opportunities can be great things currently in place in your life (e.g., a full set of vacation days remaining, a hot job market) or positive possibilities (e.g., an opening for your dream job, going back to school). Some opportunities will come and go over time, others are always there for the taking. Resources may be tangible (e.g., office space in your home, money saved up for projects) or intangible (e.g., extra time to purse goals, social media following).

What are your opportunities and resources? Remember, these are *external influences* that you typically can't control but can use to your advantage.

THREATS AND BARRIERS

Threats are the opposite of opportunities. Real or imagined, these are barriers and roadblocks that currently exist or things you fear may happen that will affect your success. Like opportunities, these are things you can't control (but you can plan for them—which we will discuss later). Some threats may be general, and shared by most people (e.g., getting cancer, losing your job) and some may be very specific to your situation. For example, a constant threat for me and my carefully laid plans is getting a migraine. Even with medication, they can lay me out for days, and if the timing is bad, it can wreak havoc on my plans and life in general.

What are your threats and barriers? Remember, these are *external influences* that you typically can't control.

Here is Cassie's completed Personal Summary Worksheet:

Personal Summary Worksheet

Personal Bio

What are your roles and responsibilities? How do you describe yourself to others? What are your most pressing issues and concerns right now?

I am a 45 year old woman - mother, wife, daughter, sister, friend. Assuming I live to be 90, I am at the midpoint of my life. Most of my time is spent with work and kid activities. I worry that the days go by so quickly and I am not enjoying the short time I have with my loved ones, especially my kids. I worry about college savings, retirement savings and staying healthy.

Internal Influences / I Can Control

Strengths & Assets

- Master's degree
- CPR certified
- Good listener (when not distracted)
- Optimistic
- Problem-solver
- Motivated to make changes
- Creative, artistic ability
- Healthy

Weaknesses & Gaps

- Not certified to teach in this state
- Not organized
- Afraid to take risks
- Sometimes passive-aggressive
- Avoid conflicts
- Prone to anxiety, especially when put on the spot or do not know anyone in a group

External Influences / I Can't Control

Opportunities & Resources

- Strong support from friends
- Have extra money saved from tax refund
- Have free time during school hours
- Local economy is growing
- Community supportive of entrepreneurs
- Stock market is going up
- Still young(ish)

Threats & Barriers

- Need flexible schedule, difficult to commit to some things I want to do
- Kids are overloaded with activities
- HVAC system is acting up
- Husband's company having layoffs
- "Office Space" type job (scary)
- Conflicts in extended family
- Difficult to network here

Now it's your turn. Find a quiet place and take a long, critical look at yourself and try to build a complete list of your strengths, weaknesses, opportunities and threats (by the way, this list is known in many organizations as a SWOT). Use extra pages if necessary.

Your Core Elements

Your life is made up of many different bits and pieces that, when combined, create a unique mosaic that provides personal meaning and value. Everyone wears a variety of different hats throughout the day. Parent, employee, sibling, colleague, friend, caretaker. The list goes on. These roles, responsibilities, duties, commitments, interests, burdens, passions and obligations make up our lives. These are our core elements—all the different pieces of our lives that make us who we are.

These are different from your values, which are abstract concepts or ideals that you hold to be true. It is good to have values and be aware of them as well, but for our purposes now, we're focusing on the tangible aspects of our lives that our planning will have a real, practical and significant effect upon.

You may have a general idea of your core elements already. Are they floating around in your head? If it isn't written down, it doesn't exist. Therefore, we will start by making them real by writing them down, then working to define and prioritize them. Often you don't really know if something is truly a priority until it is confronted with tough decisions. We will put these core elements to the test later on as we go through the planning process.

Before we get there, we need to start with a broad look at all the things in your life that are:

Important to you—things you care deeply about and prioritize above daily "noise", for example, your family's well-being, your financial security, your interests and hobbies, etc.

And/Or

Affecting you—things that you may have ambivalent or even negative feelings about, but have an impact on your life that cannot be ignored, for example, health issues, difficult relationships, lack of meaningful friendships, career uncertainties, etc.

These "things" will be grouped into broad categories that will be our starting point for understanding the big picture of *you*. These core elements of your life might be related to your family, friendships, house, work, community, finances, hobbies or other facets that make up your life. Much like the functions within a business, you can think of these as all the departments you need to run your life.

For this exercise, you will go through three steps to identify your core elements and define the unique meaning and value they hold.

ASSIGNMENT 4: IDENTIFY YOUR CORE ELEMENTS

STEP 1: BRAINSTORM

For this first step, you will need index cards or sticky notes, a timer and a clear, flat surface (I just moved the junk from my dining room table to the floor for a few minutes). If you don't have note cards, just cut up squares of paper until you have at least fifty pieces. Set your timer for five minutes. During this time, write down everything that comes to mind for the following question. *Write only one idea on each card.* Keep thinking and writing until your time is up.

What is most important to me?

Time's up. Set your cards to the side.

Next you will set your timer for another five minutes. During this time, write down everything that comes to mind for any and all of these next few questions. Remember to write only one word or phrase on each piece of paper. Keep thinking and writing until your time is up. If you need more time, feel free to take as long as you like. Five minutes should be the minimum. Cut up more paper if needed.

What would I miss most, if it were taken away?
Besides work, what do I spend my time on?
Besides basic living expenses, what do I spend my money on?
What is keeping me up at night?
What, if anything, in my life is "on hold"?

Now you should have a big pile of cards with a meaningful collection of ideas that either delight or worry you—either way, words that are relevant to you. These are the things you cherish, value and care about most in the world. Spread them all out on the table so you can gaze upon their glory for a few minutes.

As a reference, here are a few completed cards from Cassie's example. She found that the big-picture themes (e.g., health, financial security) came from answering the first question, "What is most important to me?". The important details as well as some ideas she might have missed were identified when she completed the second five-minute part.

STEP 2: SORT YOUR IDEAS INTO COMMON THEMES

What we are going to do now is called affinity mapping[11]. You will sort the cards into groups that have, well, an "affinity" for each other. You're looking for patterns in the words that suggest an underlying relationship or similarity between them. For example, if you listed out your children's names individually, they should all go together in a pile that contains "children" or maybe "family". If you listed a pet's name, like I did, you might also add that to the "family" pile. Or it could go in its own pile, if you have other pets or animals, or in the "interests" category if you consider your pet more of a hobby or interest.

Keep sorting and shuffling your cards around until you have a reasonable number of stacks, maybe seven to ten. No more than fifteen. If you have some cards that don't seem to have a place anywhere, you can put them in a stack you call the "parking lot" and come back to them later. When you're finished, the stacks should look something like this:

STEP 3: DEFINE EACH CORE ELEMENT

Each of your stacks represents a common theme. Now, think of a word or phrase that you will use to define that theme or core element. Some will be straightforward—if you listed your family members and have them together in one stack, you might name that element "Family". Others may not be so clear. You may have a collection of words that you feel belong together, but the theme is not readily apparent. Spend some time thinking about what all those cards have in common, or whether some should be re-sorted to another stack.

For example, say you have these: "sons' college tuition", "car problems", "daughter's braces" and "basement remodel". These may have come up when you answered the "what you spend your money on" or the "what keeps you up at night" questions. They may be appropriate together in one stack that you name "Finances" or "Money Related Stuff I Am Freaking Out About". Maybe just stick with "Finances". You might notice that you also have another stack having to do with home improvements, home decorating, gardening and home-related crafts. You would want to decide if the card "basement remodel" belongs in the stack you named "Home" or if it is truly a financial issue that deserves to stay in "Finances".

Cassie had trouble sorting the items "Son's grades" and "Daughter's soccer". These are things her kids (and consequently her whole family) are heavily involved in. They are important to her, and she spends a good deal of time and money on them (tutors and travel soccer are expensive!) and she would miss the soccer if it were taken away. She had them in Family at first, because they are kid-related. However, they both didn't quite fit with the "feeling" that she has when considering the Family category. For her, the family category is associated with things like spending time together during the holidays, building stronger relationships and resolving issues. Her son's grades probably fit in there pretty well as a family issue that needed resolving, but soccer didn't. She realized she associates soccer more with the social and fun aspect of the activity. She has developed good friendships with the sideline parents over the years, and her daughter has some of her best friends in that group. It made more sense to move Daughter's Soccer to an element she called "Social/Friendship".

This brings up another point—these are *your* elements—the things that you personally hold dear. Their definition should be from your perspective only. For example, if you have a fitness or health category, this should focus on *your* health and fitness. In the example above, Cassie didn't treat her daughter's soccer as a fitness item, because it didn't have anything to do with her own, personal fitness. Was she getting fit by sitting on the sideline and cheering her on and having fun with the other soccer families? No. For her, soccer is primarily a social/friendship activity, and maybe a Family activity as well, but not a Health/Fitness activity. This is your time, focus on yourself!

As you continue sorting, remember there are no right or wrong answers, this is a subjective process you do any way you want. The end goal is to come up with a name for each stack that sums up the thoughts and ideas on the cards in the stack *and* creates a full set of categories that you feel adequately captures your core elements. Here are the element names that Cassie came up with:

After you have settled on the names of each of your core elements, write them in the boxes on the Core Elements Worksheet (see example below). If you are following along on blank paper, just write them down as a list. Here is a list of some commonly used categories and alternate labels in case you're having trouble slapping a name on one. Bottom line, these need to be labels that you are comfortable with.

- Family/Close Relationships
- Career/Work/Organizations
- Religion/Faith/Spiritual Fulfillment
- Finances/Money/Financial Security

- Friendships/Social Relationships/Social Connections/Human Interactions
- Romantic Relationships/Romance/Love/Sexual Fulfillment
- Fitness/Health/Physical Health
- Mental Health/Emotional Well-Being/Self-Care
- Hobbies/Interests/Recreation/Sports/Travel
- Community Service/Volunteering/Charity/Giving Back
- Community/Neighborhood
- Learning/Education/Personal Development/Personal Growth
- Productivity/Change/Getting Stuff Done/
- Home Improvement/House/Domestic Bliss

Core Elements Worksheet

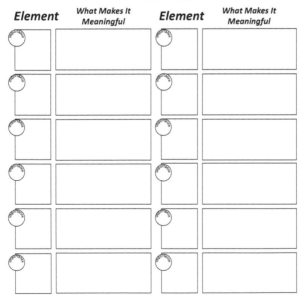

WRITE A DEFINITION FOR EACH ELEMENT

What makes each of these categories important to you? What items are in each of these categories that make it meaningful in your life? Pick the most important ideas from some of the cards in your stacks and add any other ideas that you may have left out. Using Cassie's example below (or the Core Elements Worksheet in the companion workbook), write in your elements, and describe what makes the element worthy to be included in your final Core Elements list.

When Cassie created her cards, she listed out all her family members (five minutes ends up being a lot of time to think!), both immediate and extended. She cleaned that up a little by defining "Family" as her immediate family (children and spouse), her parents, her brothers and sister and their families and her husband's sister and her family. Of course, she has aunts and uncles and cousins who are also important to her, but she felt the element should be narrowed down to only the family members that she is likely to plan her life around.

Here are some examples from Cassie's worksheet. Keep working until you have defined each of your elements.

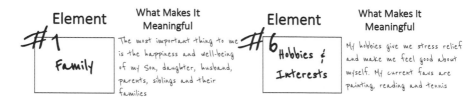

Element	What Makes It Meaningful	Element	What Makes It Meaningful
#1 Family	The most important thing to me is the happiness and well-being of my son, daughter, husband, parents, siblings and their families	#6 Hobbies & Interests	My hobbies give me stress relief and make me feel good about myself. My current favs are painting, reading and tennis

So how does that feel? Getting your thoughts and feelings down on paper can be so liberating. We walk around all day with hundreds of different thoughts jumping into and out of our consciousness. A lot of these thoughts are good ideas that disappear as soon as some other thought pops in. When we're trying to make critical choices, some of these thoughts may be right there in the forefront to help us decide, whereas others may be hidden in our memories, only to appear after the choice is already made.

Writing this down can also be frustrating. You might not be able to come up with enough things to make a category meaningful. That could come as a surprise, especially if you have been holding that category up as one of your core values in life. An example might be Learning & Education—you put it down as an important part of your life, but perhaps you can't think of one relevant thing to add. Or perhaps the things you are thinking have completely changed your idea of what that category means to you.

BINGO! It might be a key goal that has for whatever reason been pushed to the back burner for years. For example, you might not have completed any substantial actions that support your own learning, but you know it is something you want to do. Or your thinking is shifting and now that you've written it down, you're aware of it for the first time. Congratulations! Leave that empty or confusing bucket there for now, and you will work on it more when you start creating your Master Plan.

Your Priorities

ASSIGNMENT 5: PRIORITIZE YOUR CORE ELEMENTS

The last assignment in *Part 1: Look Around* is to prioritize your core elements. I get easily agitated by illogical or overly complicated surveys and questionnaires with too many options, complex ranking systems and confusing instructions. I tried hard to keep this exercise as simple as possible. Here's what this step boils down to—rank order your elements by how important they are to you.

Pull out your Core Elements Worksheet again. Look back over your elements. Remind yourself why they are meaningful to you. Now, pick the element that is the most important to you at this moment in time. Don't over-think it. This doesn't have to be difficult, just let your eyes rest on your number one most critical life element, then write a big old #1 beside the box.

All good? Now pick your second most important element. Label it #2. Now continue through the list. No whining allowed. Don't try to give anything a 1.5 or pull any "these two are tied" business. Just rank order your elements from one to whatever and be done with it. If you need help defining what "important" means, you're over-thinking it.

Here is Cassie's completed example:

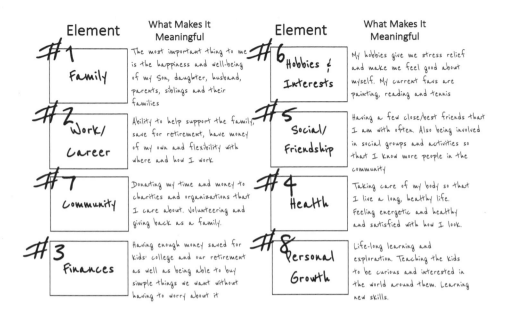

Element	What Makes It Meaningful	Element	What Makes It Meaningful
#1 Family	The most important thing to me is the happiness and well-being of my son, daughter, husband, parents, siblings and their families	#6 Hobbies & Interests	My hobbies give me stress relief and make me feel good about myself. My current favs are painting, reading and tennis
#2 Work/Career	Ability to help support the family, save for retirement, have money of my own and flexibility with where and how I work	#5 Social/Friendship	Having a few close/best friends that I am with often. Also being involved in social groups and activities so that I know more people in the community
#7 Community	Donating my time and money to charities and organizations that I care about. Volunteering and giving back as a family.	#4 Health	Taking care of my body so that I live a long, healthy life. Feeling energetic and healthy and satisfied with how I look.
#3 Finances	Having enough money saved for kids' college and our retirement as well as being able to buy simple things we want without having to worry about it	#8 Personal Growth	Life-long learning and exploration. Teaching the kids to be curious and interested in the world around them. Learning new skills.

Why be so adamant about ranking? In order to tackle some of your hardest decisions in the most efficient way, you must be able to prioritize them. You can't do everything at once, so focus on the things that are most important in your life. This is one of the biggest mistakes we make and also happens to be our most convenient excuse when nothing gets done—we just don't have the time to do all the things. Well guess what? Of course, you don't, and you never will have the time to do all the things. No one does. Prioritization is where we start picking out the important, valuable things we can do and want to do, and doing them. Then moving on to the less important things. You will have more opportunities to prioritize and move things around later.

Okay, that's the end of this part of the program. You now hold in your hands the snapshot of each of your elements, prioritized and ready for you to start setting goals and writing plans so that each one will get better and better. I recommend taking a break at this point to let the ideas gel in your subconscious, then come back in a day or so refreshed and ready to work.

PART TWO TAKEAWAYS:

- Before making plans for the future, you must get a clear and accurate understanding of your current reality.

- Be crystal-clear about the most important areas of your life—your Core Elements. Your goals will be focused on improving each of these elements.

- Prioritization is the key to getting things done.

PART THREE: LOOK AHEAD

Where do you want to go? Who do you want to be? How do you get unstuck from your current situation and move toward your ideal? The first step will be to create a guiding vision that defines what your perfect future looks like. Next you will set goals that link directly to that vision, each of which will be based on your Core Elements, the aspects of your life that you prioritized as key to your happiness and success. Finally, you will build a Master Plan around the goals that define the actions and choices you will make going forward.

Your Guiding Vision

You want to live a more fulfilling life, you recognize the need for constant renewal and growth, you feel the urge to do better, to change, to adapt, to thrive. The first step for addressing both the short-term goals and the long-term dreams for your life is to create a guiding vision.

Your guiding vision is a key part of what enables you to recognize important choices and choose the right one. Either a choice aligns with your vision (i.e., good choice) or it doesn't (i.e., bad choice).

It is difficult to see past the reality of today with all its demands, stress, bad news, worry, deadlines and anxiety and envision a different future. You may be so constrained by your situation that you don't see any other choices out there. All you may see are the roadblocks. You feel locked in by your own history, your age, your education, your recent experiences or financial commitments. External factors may also be relevant, such as the limited job opportunities you see online, or other people talking about "how bad things are these days". Maybe adult peer pressure is getting to you—what will my friends think? Will this make me look stupid? What if I fail? Maybe it is just the fact you've been doing this one thing for so long, you can't imagine doing anything else.

Your task in this assignment is to shift yourself out of today's world. You already got those ideas down in the SWOT. If there are still some that are bugging you, go back and put them down on paper and out of your mind. Now you can think openly and freely about the world that you want, the difference you want to make, and the best way that you can make the most of the time you have. You're not going to think about how or whether to quit your job, change careers, make more money, have more time, lose weight or how to fix any of the other problems of your reality right now. You are going to start by focusing on big-picture possibilities and defining your ideal life.

Consider these guiding visions. These organizations each have drawn a clear line in the sand and defined their primary direction. Their goals, actions and investments—*the choices they make as an organization*—drive them toward their visions. But they had to define the vision first—before they could make any of the subsequent decisions.

- **Smithsonian**—Shaping the future by preserving our heritage, discovering new knowledge, and sharing our resources with the world (https://www.si.edu/about/mission)

- **ASCPA**—The vision of the ASCPA is that the United States is a humane community in which all animals are treated with respect and kindness (https://www.aspca.org/about-us/aspca-policy-and-position-statements/vision)

- **VFW (Veterans of Foreign Wars)**—Ensure that veterans are respected for their service, always receive their earned entitlements, and are recognized for the sacrifices they and their loved ones have made on behalf of this great country (https://www.vfw.org/about-us)

ASSIGNMENT 6: DEFINE YOUR GUIDING VISION

A vision statement is a written description of the idealized view of your future, the best possible outcome that you can imagine for your life. Your vision should define the best possible *you*, the you who has become everything you are capable of becoming. The purpose of having a vision statement is to show you the path ahead and inspire and energize you to move forward.

You will never be greater than the vision that guides you.

Your vision statement, if truly inspirational, should push you out of your comfort zone. Don't hold back, and don't be embarrassed by putting your ideas down on paper. No one has to see this but you (but when you get it right, you may want to share it with everyone).

The perfect statement rarely materializes quickly. You may find it takes several tries over the course of days to get a statement that truly reflects your ideal vision. Although the vision should be a fairly stable idea over time, you may find that it requires slight tweaks and additions over the years as your life circumstances change.

STEP 1: VISUALIZE YOUR FUTURE SELF

Close your eyes and picture yourself ten years from now. Say your age out loud. Let that settle in for a second.

How do you look? Don't just say "ten years older", really try to picture yourself in ten years. What physical differences will you see? Where are you? This can be your physical location as well as where you are in your career, life stage, social group, etc. How do you feel? Who are you with? What are you doing? What types of things are surrounding you?

Now with you at the same point in your future, imagine what your world looks like if everything were absolutely "ideal". There are no barriers, no roadblocks, no limits to your potential. Imagine that starting today, you used the next ten years to do every single thing you wanted to do with your life. Now, you are ten years down the road and you abso-freaking-lutely nailed that decade.

STEP 2: WRITE DOWN THE KEY IDEAS

With that vision in mind, write your answers to the following:

- How do you feel?
- How do you look?
- Where are you?
- Who are you with?
- What are you doing?
- What are you surrounded by?
- What are you most proud of at this point in your life?

What changed between your first mental picture of your future, and the "perfected" one? What are the key aspects of yourself that improved or changed? What are aspects of your life and world that have changed? Write a summary of the key ideas and phrases that best encapsulate this future ideal *you.*

STEP 3: CREATE YOUR VISION STATEMENT

Now, turn this vision of your future self into a clear statement of your ideals, your priorities, and your idea of life success. The final statement needs to be just *a few sentences* (aim for fifty words or less) that are inspirational and ambitious, yet realistic and reflects the authentic *you.* Write your statement as if it is happening now (in present tense if you remember that from high school English class) so that you can feel yourself there, in that ideal state. Be sure you are describing the ideal state, and not the steps to get there. Finally, check your statement against the following criteria:

INSPIRATIONAL	You read it and you want to be there. It draws you in and makes you feel the urge to move in that direction. It's a shining beacon guiding you forward.
AMBITIOUS	It requires you to work hard, to get up and get moving. It is a vision that is not just going to happen, you know it will take sweat and tears, but will be so worth it!
HIGH-LEVEL	This is the place to establish the "why"—why do I exist in this world? What is my purpose? Where am I heading? This is the place to say, "I want to be healthy", not "I want to lose ten pounds" or "run a marathon". There is a time and place for those

awesome goals, but this is not it. Keep it up in the clouds.

REALISTIC — Your vision must be something that you can accomplish. Your vision should in no way set you up to fail (let's face it, as much as I like to look at the stars, at this point in my life I don't think there is any chance I'll become an astronaut). If there is even a chance though, that it could happen, feel free to throw it out there. The successes along the way to your pie-in-the-sky idea may just be the end result that you really wanted anyway.

SHORT AND CRYSTAL-CLEAR — This is not the place to start planning the "what and how", that will come with your plan. Communicate your vision in one short, concise statement that screams off the page as your vision of your future.

Sometimes the first few words are the hardest. Don't sweat them for now, you can refine this later. Pick one or more to start your sentences.

- I am...
- I have...
- I am able to...
- I can...
- I no longer...
- I am proud to say that I am...
- I have made my parents/spouse/family proud by...
- I have earned my degree in...
- I have a satisfying relationship with...

- I am happy and content with my...
- I am respected in my community/organization/field for...
- I am a recognized expert in...

You can write and re-write your statement as much as you need. Sometimes it helps take a break and come back after a good night's sleep to make your adjustments. This is not an easy task. Don't feel bad if it doesn't sound perfect right away.

VISION STATEMENT EXAMPLES

Here is an example of a vision statement draft and final version. Note the slight adjustments that made the statement more compelling.

First Draft Example ⟹	Improved
In ten years, I should be able to run a marathon and write a book and be happy. I also hope to have a better relationship with my sister and my kids should be happy and give back to society.	I am physically fit and feel great! I have a job that I love to get up for in the morning, and I am an expert my field. I have strong and loving relationships with my family and I am a volunteer in my community.
• Not inspiring • Too many "whats", not enough high-level aspirations • Rambling, unclear who the vision is for • Difficult to communicate • May not be realistic	• Inspiring • Clear • Ambitious • High-level enough to accommodate different goals as your life changes over time

In the examples, you can see how taking the raw ideas presented on the left and tweaking them creates a better statement. Asking "why" for thoughts such as "run a marathon" and "write a book" yield the real dream sitting behind those actions. If you feel your statement is too tactical, ask yourself "why?" for each idea you included. In this case, the "why" behind "marathon" is really a desire to be physically fit enough to complete something as grueling as a marathon. The actual race can then be part of the larger plan to achieve this aspirational goal but is too specific to be in the vision. For one thing, it's limiting. If you run the marathon, then what? Are you finished? Do you have to rewrite your vision? Not if you keep the vision open and high-level enough. The marathon may be but one step on your journey to a lifetime of physical fitness and health.

Being too specific can also cause you to miss where your heart really wants to lead you. Your brain may be stuck on "write a book", but what you really, truly want is to be viewed as an expert on a topic and writing a book may or may not be the best way to get there. Again, the planning phase of this program is where you will work out all those details. For now, put the dreams down on paper and hold off on specific ideas.

To make your statement more clear and concise, try consolidating some thoughts into the larger ideas they represent. For example, to simplify the complex tasks of working through issues with a sibling or supporting your child in ways that helps them improve their academic achievement, health or well-being, look for the central idea that supports these activities. It might boil down to developing stronger relationships with them. Or you could include a statement about providing support and resources for them to achieve their own goals. Again, your vision is not the place for detailed actions.

Here are some additional examples that may help get your ideas flowing.

I am healthy, productive and joyful in my life, while supporting and nurturing my family, friends and community	I am leaving things better than I found them, everywhere I go and with everything I do	I am joyfully living a life that is active, creative, and fun, surrounded by those I love and free from cancer
• Powerful • High-level • Clear • Sounds good spoken out loud	• Aspirational • Ambitious • Achievable • Concise	• Emotionally stirring • Creates a clear picture in your mind

Now that you have the first working draft of your vision in hand—keep it there! Print it out, paint it on the wall, cut out a fancy vinyl with your Silhouette/Cricut machine and stick it to something. Whatever, just make sure your vision statement is always within sight. You should be able to rattle it off without even thinking. It is your own personal tagline.

Your Goals and Choices

Vision without action is merely a dream. Action without vision just passes the time. Vision with action can change the world.

-Joel A. Barker

Okay, keep that vision out where you can see it. Now you are going to start setting specific goals that will, over time, make your vision a reality. Remember those Core Elements you created earlier? Get those out too. In this part of the program, you will take a deep dive into each of the elements and think about all the things you would do to make each of those facets of your life exceptional, if only you had the time, resources and energy. Much like the vision exercise, this is not the time to dwell on all the roadblocks and harsh realities that may be jumping in and out of your field of view as you try to see your future self. This is your chance to put down on paper each of the fabulous things that will contribute to the new future, the one just described in your vision.

Review your Core Elements page—look again at each of the categories, and all the things that you place within each. Think about the importance you assigned to each. In this task, you'll work your way through each of the elements, starting with the one you ranked most important.

Consider the hopes, dreams and high-level aspirations you have for each of these elements. You will brainstorm all the things that you might do to achieve those dreams. The steps in this assignment are iterative— as you work through them, expect to go back and forth as each idea builds on and improves other related elements and goals. There are four steps in this exercise. A warning, it may take a few work sessions to finish this one. It is worth it though!

ASSIGNMENT 7: SET YOUR GOALS AND PLAN YOUR CHOICES

STEP 1: BRAINSTORM POTENTIAL GOALS

On a big, blank sheet of paper, write your name and vision statement in the middle and put a box around it. You are the center of this universe. We'll use our friend Cassie's vision as an example.

ME

I am healthy and productive, enjoying my job, and supporting and nurturing my family, friends and community

Next, draw one line coming out of the circle, in any direction. This is called a mental diagram or a "mind map". We're eventually going to create a picture that looks like a big wheel, with the hub (you and your guiding vision) in the center, and your Core Elements as the spokes that fan out in all directions. For now, just start with one of those elements. At the end of the spoke, write down one of your highest-importance elements. Your page should look something like this:

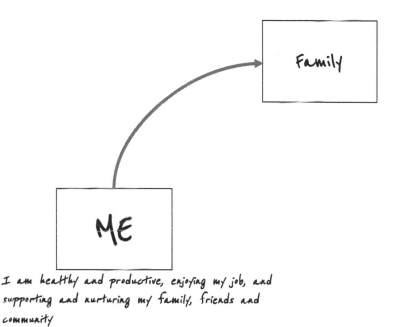

I am healthy and productive, enjoying my job, and supporting and nurturing my family, friends and community

Look back at how you defined this element—these are all the things you placed in there that make it meaningful to you. For example, if you chose Family for the first one, who and what did you place in that element? Visualize those people, things or places for a moment. What are some of the needs, wishes, and goals you have for them? What do you want the relationships to be in the future? Are there problems that need to be addressed? Conflicts that need to be resolved? Perhaps the relationships are healthy, but you see opportunities to strengthen them. Does that involve time? Resources? Specific activities or tasks that need to be done?

This is where you will begin to formulate the ideas that will eventually become goals for each of the elements of your life. Ask:

- What do you want to happen in this element?
- What are some things that need to change or improve?
- What potential results, solutions or outcomes do you envision?

Some find it helpful to start with a "mini-vision" for the element. In this case, Cassie's mini-vision for her Family element is "to have a happy, strong, tightly-connected family". From that idea, define what that would look like, for example, a happy, strong and tightly-connect family might be one that "communicates openly and often", "sees each other often", "resolves conflicts", "does fun stuff together", "treats each other well", etc. From each of these ideas, you can start to write goals. Taking the "sees each other often" idea for example, think about what that would entail. Cassie came up with the more specific goal of "see parents more". For "does fun stuff together", she refined to "spend more quality time with the kids".

These are ideas for brainstorming your goals. You may already have some specific things in mind, or you may need to spend some time sketching out ideas and refining them. Either way, write them down right there on the paper beside the element. You may have one thing, you may have one hundred.

Feel free to use a separate sheet of paper for each element if needed.

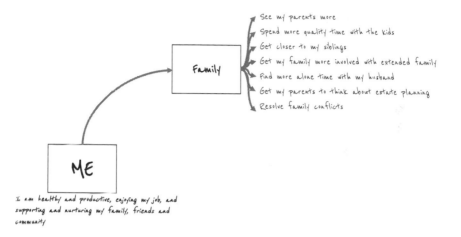

See my parents more
Spend more quality time with the kids
Get closer to my siblings
Get my family more involved with extended family
Find more alone time with my husband
Get my parents to think about estate planning
Resolve family conflicts

Family

ME

I am healthy and productive, enjoying my job, and supporting and nurturing my family, friends and community

Don't waste time trying to make this pretty. Save the artistry for your bullet journal or sketchbook, just get the ideas down on paper. Previously, for the Core Element Cassie called "Family", she included her husband, kids, parents, sister, brothers, their families and in-laws. That is what constitutes "Family" for her.

The first few should be easy. If you have a spouse or significant other, chances are you need to work to keep that relationship strong or address issues in the relationship. Spending more time together might be one goal to do that. If you have children, that can be more difficult, so your goal might be more specific—"spending more alone time with significant other". Creating tighter connections and resolving conflicts are common goals, as are starting/expanding family or finding a special someone. Other Family goals might be targeted at specific issues and will start to come to mind as you continue to think.

Cassie's parents are getting older, and as one of five children, she would like to know that they have thought through how her and her siblings are supposed to handle things when they are gone. Touchy subject. She realized as she was going through this process that she didn't even know if they have a will in place. She made it a top priority goal for the year to find out. Another one from her example is a more recent issue, but one that is growing and is troubling her quite a bit—conflicts between two of her brothers. She wrote down "resolve family conflicts"—she is not necessarily going to be able to fix it, but it's now on her radar screen to try to help them. During the planning part coming up, she can decide whether "fix" is the right idea or not. For now, just get the ideas down, they can be tweaked and massaged later.

Before moving on to the next element, look back at your vision. Is there anything in your vision statement that directly focuses on this element? If so, what are some of the things you might do to get yourself closer to that ideal vision? Cassie must look at her goals for her Family Core Element *through the lens of her vision statement*—specifically the part about supporting and nurturing her family. Each goal should link in some way to that idea in the vision. It's usually not hard to make the link, but if you do find that one of your goals is truly not related to your vision in any way, you need to take a step back. Either the goal is not in line with your future vision and should probably be deleted or changed so that it fits, or your vision is missing a key element that you still desire for your future and it needs to be updated.

Continue filling in your elements and the high-level raw goals for each on your paper. It will begin to look like this:

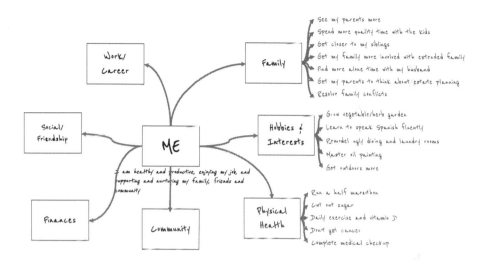

Keep going with this until each of your elements is completely full of goals, and your brain is empty. It should feel great to get all these ideas that have been bottled up in your mind down on paper. It may be a hot mess right now. We have some steps coming up to help refine the ideas into a streamlined, actionable plan.

STEP 2: PRIORITIZE YOUR RAW GOALS

The trick to getting control over your choices is acting on the important information and ignoring the noise. Get into the habit of approaching your goals and choices in a thoughtful, structured manner, rather than just attacking each thing as it comes at you. Prioritization is your secret weapon.

Another reason to prioritize is to avoid a big mistake people often make when changing anything about their lives—trying to accomplish too many things at once. You can insert any of a number of clichés here—boiling the ocean, eating an elephant, etc. Can you boil the ocean? No, but you can boil one pot of water at a time. Can you eat a whole elephant? You probably shouldn't, but if you really wanted to, but you could cut the poor thing up and eat a little bit at a time. Okay, extreme examples, whatever, just don't try to do it all at once. Narrow down your ideas into a few that you can do now. Complete those and hit the next ones. No one is saying you can't do them all, you just can't do them all at once. So, here is where you start to prioritize.

There are several different ways you can prioritize things, but I like to keep two main things in mind: How much the action is going to benefit me, and how much time/cost/effort it's going to take to do it. The combination of those two things tells me what to tackle first (or at all). If the overall cost is more than the benefit that comes from it, it isn't a worthwhile goal. I know it feels more complicated than that when you are in the thick of it, but it's usually not.

This is where the rubber meets the road for most decisions: What is it going to cost me versus what will I get out of it?

COST VERSUS BENEFIT

Impact (Benefit)—this is the "what's in it for me" side of the equation. For the goals you have listed, answer the following:

- Will accomplishing this goal make a difference in my life?
- Will it directly help me to move closer to my guiding vision?
- Is it urgent that this gets done now, or can it wait?
- If this doesn't happen right away, what are the consequences?

If the goal will make a big difference in your life or help you move forward in a positive direction, or aligns directly with your vision, then the benefit is going to be higher. If the goal is either not impactful, or you think it will provide only a moderate or slight benefit, then the benefit will be lower.

Difficulty (Cost)—this is the "how much time, effort, money, etc." side of the equation. For the goals you have written, answer the following:

- How much time and effort will it take to complete this goal?
- Will I need money or other resources to do it? Do I have this available right now, or will I have to make a plan for obtaining resources?
- Is this something I can do myself, or will I need help and cooperation from other people?
- Is this a "one and done" goal, or will it take continued effort to ensure it succeeds? For example, a one-time goal might be a dream trip to Europe, whereas a weight-loss goal will be a long-term goal that requires continued

effort. Typically, the one-time goals will be easier to complete, even if the up-front cost is higher.

If you put these two ideas together, you get a prioritization grid that looks like this:

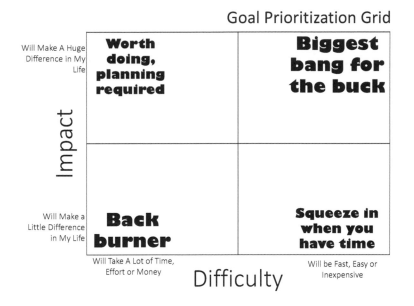

Goal Prioritization Grid

Will Make A Huge Difference in My Life	**Worth doing, planning required**	**Biggest bang for the buck**
Will Make a Little Difference in My Life	**Back burner**	**Squeeze in when you have time**
	Will Take A Lot of Time, Effort or Money	Will be Fast, Easy or Inexpensive

Impact

Difficulty

The right column should contain what you feel are the easiest, fastest, lowest-cost goals and left column should be the most difficult, most expensive and/or most time-consuming ones. The top row should contain the most significant, impactful and urgent actions on your list, and the bottom row should contain the least impactful ones. It should be pretty easy to see which ones you should tackle first (hint—"biggest bang for the buck").

At this point your goals are raw. After you prioritize, you will refine your highest priority goals into actionable statements and then plan for their completion. So, looking at your first raw goal, decide what sort of impact it will have on achieving your vision (using the questions under the Impact definition above). Then decide if it will be easy or difficult to complete, using the questions under Difficulty. Depending on these ratings, write that goal in the grid. For example, Cassie's first goal within her Family element was "see my parents more". The questions she asked herself were:

- Will accomplishing this goal make a difference in my life?

- *Yes, it would make me happy to spend a big chunk of time with them rather than the short, sporadic visits we have had for the past few years. I assume it would also make them happy.*

- Will it directly affect me in achieving my vision?

- *Yes, it aligns with the "supporting and nurturing my family" portion of my vision.*

- Is it urgent that this gets done now, or can it wait?

- *Summer is the only time that I can get off work long enough to go, and the only time the kids can go. We could possibly wait until next summer, but I would rather not.*

- If this doesn't happen right away, what would happen?

- *My parents are healthy and active right now, but as we all know, our lives can change at any time. I would have enormous regrets if I didn't go when I had the chance and then the opportunity was lost if something happened to one of us.*

Based on these answers, her rating for the first factor of Impact is the highest it can be. This goal could have a significant impact on her Family element and is directly related to her vision.

On to the second factor, Difficulty. Cassie's answers for this factor are:

- How much time and effort will it take to complete this goal?

- *Two weeks off work in addition to the effort of scheduling the trip, searching for and buying plane tickets, travel to and from the airports and keeping the kids occupied while we are away from home for two weeks. That plus any other visits, I would say a moderate amount of effort.*

- Will I need money or other resources to do it?

- *I will definitely need money to make this happen, as plane tickets are expensive. Even if I drive, it will require an overnight stay in a hotel, so the price of the trip will be what I consider a moderate amount of money.*

- Do I have this available right now, or will I have to make a plan for obtaining resources?

- *No, so even if I charge it on my credit card, I will be able to afford the cost without additional actions. I would classify this one as moderate to easy.*

- Is this something I can do myself, or will I need help and cooperation from other people?

- *I can do this mostly by myself but would like to have the support of my husband since I feel bad that he will probably not be able to join us. I also need to make sure my parents are okay with the idea, but I do not foresee any problems here. Easy.*

- Is this a "one and done" goal, or will it take continued effort to ensure it succeeds?
- *It depends, it will probably be a combination of both.*

Based on her answers, she would put this task near the middle for the difficulty, leaning toward the left (more difficult) column. Taking both of these together, the prioritization looks something like this:

As you continue to work through your goals from your mind map, your prioritization grid will begin to fill up with what is now a prioritized collection of goals—the beginning of your Master Plan! If it gets too crowded, you may want to use on grid per element. As Cassie went through the thought process of evaluating the Impact and Difficulty of the goals she was proposing, she found that some of them changed focus, some were combined, and some new ones were added. She also struggled to keep all the goals out of the upper part of the grid. It's important that you try to distribute them throughout the grid, especially across Impact. Acknowledge that everything cannot possibly have the same impact—some goals will affect your life more than others, and the grid needs to reflect those differences to be useful to you. Likewise, the difficulty of completing them is likely to vary as well, and the grid should show this variation.

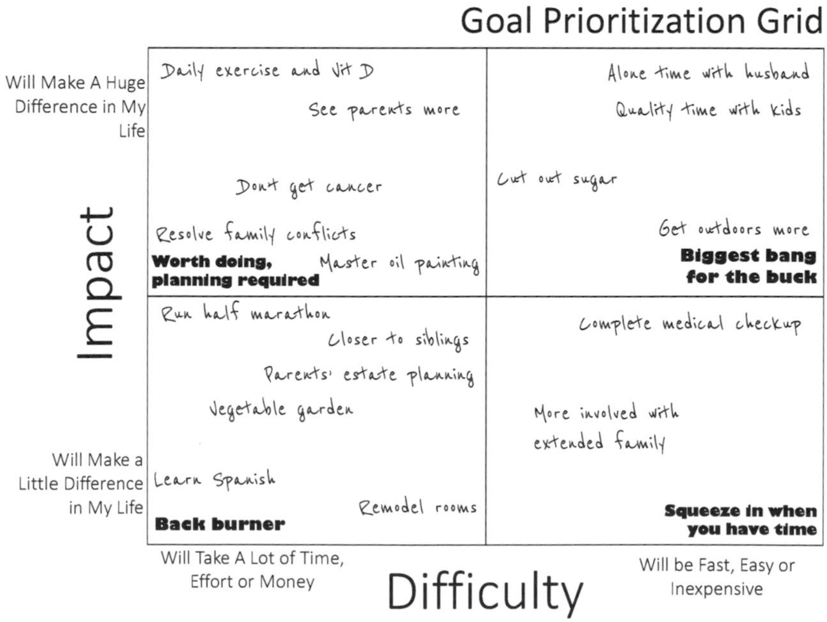

Goal Prioritization Grid

	Will Take A Lot of Time, Effort or Money	Will be Fast, Easy or Inexpensive
Will Make A Huge Difference in My Life	Daily exercise and Vit D / See parents more / Don't get cancer / Resolve family conflicts / Master oil painting / **Worth doing, planning required**	Alone time with husband / Quality time with kids / Cut out sugar / Get outdoors more / **Biggest bang for the buck**
Will Make a Little Difference in My Life	Run half marathon / Closer to siblings / Parents' estate planning / Vegetable garden / Learn Spanish / Remodel rooms / **Back burner**	Complete medical checkup / More involved with extended family / **Squeeze in when you have time**

Impact (vertical axis) — **Difficulty** (horizontal axis)

ALMOST THERE! PRIORITIZATION SHORTHAND

You can assign a priority code to each box on the grid that will make crystal-clear the order these actions should be done.

The grid illustrates the priority. The letter provides the importance of this goal.

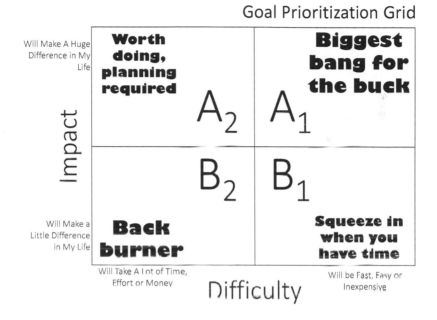

The top right box is the sweet spot on your grid. These give you the "biggest bang for the buck"—huge impact, but fast and easy to accomplish with little cost or effort on your part. These should be the ones you go after first. Get them done and out of the way and start reaping the benefits of action! For the rest of the boxes, here is the general order of execution you should follow:

- A1's should be completed first. They provide the most return for the smallest investment of time and effort. If you have a lot of these, you can use your Master Plan to schedule them, so you don't get overwhelmed.

- A2's are the next most important goals, but because they are more difficult to complete, they will need to be prioritized within the A2 group and tackled one at a time. Although not covered in this book, more substantial project management tools may be useful.

- B1's should be completed after the A1's and when time permits you to fit them around your A2's. Remember, these are quick and easy to do, but should not get in the way of getting some of your more important A goals accomplished. B's can be important goals too, but their priority is pushed down because they aren't making an enormous impact on your vision.

- B2's are the nice-to-haves that you can save for later. They may be items that become important or more interesting later on as other goals are completed, or they may be ones that fade and disappear after a while. Review them periodically to see if they need to be reprioritized (or deleted).

STEP 3: WRITE CLEAR GOAL STATEMENTS

Now that you know what your top priorities are, you're going to turn back to your goals and refine them so that they are straightforward and simple and contain enough information to guide you to success. Each goal will take a little effort to write, so for now, focus on the A goals. You can move to the B's next, but most of your effort should be spent on getting those top-priority goals clear in your mind. To the extent possible, your written goals should tell you "who, what, when, where, why and how much". The following three concepts will help you fit it all into a clear statement:

WRITE GOAL STATEMENTS THAT ARE:

- ACTIONABLE: This is the *what, where and who*. Make your goal actionable by describing the specific thing that will be done by a specific person or group of people, and where (if applicable) this will take place.

- IMPORTANT: This is the *why*. The goal should support your vision, so think about how this goal relates. Explain why it is motivating, significant and meaningful to you.

- MEASURABLE: This is the *when and how much*. Make your goal measurable by setting a timeframe or deadline for its completion, and what success will look like.

Here is an example. Cassie started with a raw goal of what she wanted to happen in general (see parents more). By thinking through these three concepts, she expanded that into an actionable, important and measurable goal.

RAW GOAL: *See my parents more*

ACTIONABLE

- What do I want? Cassie decided: *To see my parents more.*

- Is there anything more specific to add to that? Does "seeing" them mean being together in person? You may have to do a little soul-searching here. Cassie decided: *I want the goal to be focused on being with them, in person, hugs and meals and watching TV together and talking and doing stuff together.* To better explain her "What", she replaced "see" with "spend time together"

- Who is involved in this goal? Are there any people or groups that are relevant for this goal? Cassie said: *My parents, but also me and my kids. It's not that my husband doesn't like my parents, but I can't factor his available vacation days into this goal, so I have to leave him out. He will join us when he can.*

- Where will this take place? Is location a key factor? Cassie decided: *Location may come into play during the planning phase for this goal, but for now it is not relevant.* Some goals will be quite dependent on place, for example goals around traveling to specific places or getting into a specific college, etc. For others, it may not matter.

IMPORTANT

- Why is this goal important to me? Cassie's thoughts were: *It is important to me because I love spending time with my parents and I know in my heart that time with them is fleeting. They are healthy now but won't be forever (neither will I for that matter). I would like to spend this healthy time we have now, having fun and doing stuff and making more memories for me, them and my kids.* She summed up this sentiment by starting her goal statement with, "In order to keep us strongly connected"

MEASURABLE

- What does success look like? Is success an amount? A deadline? A quality? In other words, how will you know when you have reached this goal? Perhaps it is that a deadline is met, or a certain quantity of goodness acquired, or a threshold for some target happiness reached. Cassie reasoned: *In the original goal, I only have the word "more". If I saw them X number of days last year, I could set a number of days that is higher, and a target timeframe for completion—in this case let's say twenty-eight days over the course of one calendar year.* That means Cassie has given herself two measures for her goal: how much (four weeks) and by when (deadline is December 31).

GOAL STATEMENT: *To keep us strongly connected, the kids, my parents and I will spend at least twenty-eight days together during this calendar year.*

Continue this process for all of your goals. Use the Goal Statement Worksheet from the companion workbook or create your own (see example below) to help you get started. After you do this a few times, you'll get the hang of it and be able to write them in your sleep. At this point, you should have a good list of goals started on either your mind map or in a list organized by Core Element. They should be refined so they are actionable, important and measurable.

Goal Statement Worksheet

Original Goal:	
Actionable • What do I want? • Who is involved in this goal? Are there any people or groups I need to consider? • Where will this take place? Is location a key factor?	
Important • What problem will this goal solve? • Why is this goal important to me? • How does it related to my guiding vision?	
Measurable • What does success look like? • When would I like to complete this goal?	
Improved Goal:	

Step 4: Turn Your Goals Into CHOICES

A common reason people aren't able to reach their goals is they don't know the behaviors needed to achieve them[12]. The next step is to start breaking each of your goals down into the *actual choices* you will make to work toward the goal. Starting with your high-priority goals, think about how it might be broken into smaller steps that can be taken to achieve it. Go back to your mind map and jot down the choices you will need to make to achieve each goal. Each of the goals may end up with several choices that look like this:

As you go through, expect to re-write and refine your planned choices/actions. You may refine the sentences, so they are clearer, and add details to fill out the idea. Many times, the actions will be interconnected, so you may end up combining the ideas into single actions or breaking apart ones that contain too many ideas. The actions you come up with may, in some cases, alter the meaning of the goal. That is okay, nothing is set in stone, so take a step back and rework the goal so that it makes sense for you.

Cassie's first raw goal on her mind map, which was simply "see parents more" has grown to "To keep us strongly connected, the kids and I and my parents will spend at least twenty-eight days together during this calendar year". Now, as she thinks about the tasks involved in meeting that goal, it's getting broader (for example, are there options other than being in the same location that would count as spending time together?). This has opened her mind to different options for connecting with them. Her choices include visiting in person (choosing to take time off work and travel to see them over the summer) as well as "spending time" by choosing to follow through consistently on weekly video and phone calls. She went back to her goals and put quotes around "together" to remind her that "together" can mean different types of choices. Note: It may be necessary to tweak the prioritization of a goal after adding choices, as the difficulty may change.

The next tool to organize the information from the mind map, prioritization grid and goals and choices brainstorming exercise is the Goals to Choices Worksheet. The following example shows Cassie's completed Family Element. These are the refined goal statements, and the choices she will need to make to achieve the goal. Here is Cassie's example of the Goals to Choices Worksheet with prioritization column filled in.

Goals to Choices Worksheet

Priority	Core Element	Goal	Choices
A2	Family	To keep us strongly connected, the kids, my parents and I will spend at least 28 days together during this year	• Spend two weeks with them this summer • Force them to do video calls with kids • Invite them to visit in the fall • Call 3x per week during day (short chat)
A1	Family	Of the "free time" we have between school and bed time each day, one hour of that should be focused 100% on the kids	• Weekly family game night (Monday) • Eat dinner together as a family every weeknight • Screens/devices away during devoted time • Have one favorite show we watch together
B1	Family	To keep us connected with my extended family, we should "see" each other at least 12 times this year	• Plan one visit every 2 months • Video call with all the kids weekly • Put kids in charge of birthday cards
A1	Family	To keep relationship strong, we need to spend at least 15 minutes alone each day and do something together alone once per week	• Date night with husband once per month, no kids • Walk the dog with husband alone every evening • Do treadmill while he is working out

Now it's your turn. Complete a Goals to Choices Worksheet for each of your Core Elements. This exercise is the first iteration of what is a continuous cycle of planning and improvement. The prioritization of your goals will change, just as the priorities in your life change. Things happen that push some goals to the back-burner and bring some things to the forefront. As you achieve goals, others will step up to take their place, and their very nature may be changed by the achievement of the previous goal. The next step in the program, finalizing your Master Plan, will help you keep track of all these great things you're going to do.

Your Master Plan

So, what is the "Master Plan" exactly? The common definition of a master plan is a comprehensive, far-reaching plan of action. Commonly used in city and community planning, a master plan provides the guidance that determines how a community will make decisions on things like roads, utilities, recreation, housing and generally how an area of land is used. It has a long-term time horizon, is put in place early on, and can guide land use decisions for decades. Ideally, your Master Plan will work in a similar way. You put the framework in place, and make changes and additions as your life changes, year after year.

Your Master Plan is the tool that ties all of the planning we have done so far together and drives your whole set of choices toward meeting your goals, and your goals toward achieving your vision. You have already completed the bulk of the work. Now all you have to do is organize your assignment notes and goals into the final plan.

This is also the point in this program that you may want to break from paper and pencil and transfer your planning over into an electronic tool. As much as I am a believer in physically writing ideas down on paper, it has taken you as far as it can. Due to the ever-changing nature of your list, and the sheer amount of information it will contain, an Excel spreadsheet or table in Word, or one of the many productivity apps available will be the most efficient way to manage the plan from this point on. You will be tracking your goals, choices and tasks to completion, and constantly adding and sorting the list as you work through your items. For anyone who regularly uses to-do lists to manage everyday tasks, you may already have a tool you're comfortable with. Assuming most people have access to a standard spreadsheet software package and are reasonably adept at using it, we'll start with that. If you would rather stick with pencil and paper, that's perfectly fine as well.

ASSIGNMENT 8: WRITE YOUR MASTER PLAN

STEP 1: PICK YOUR TOOL

There are several ways that you can do this, and not knowing exactly what your preference or your comfort and access to technology is, I'm going to give you a few different options. I'll give you my way of doing it first. I use a combination of electronic tools (Excel mostly) and paper. Call me a Luddite if you want, but I have this beloved binder that I print and store all of my plans and lists in from all the years I've done this. Holding that object in my hand gives my goals (past, present and future) a physical presence. Maybe it makes them feel more real, I don't know. And having it printed out just makes me happy.

I still have a list I called "Goals and Guidelines for my Lifetime" that I wrote when I was twenty-two years old. I wish I could give my twenty-two-year-old self a big hug right now for having such high aspirations. She/I didn't hit all of them, not yet anyway. Or even most of them, there are 115 things on this list and some are pretty funny in hindsight (e.g., bench press my body weight ten times (why??) and own a lava lamp (must have been going through my 1990's neo-hippie phase)). But what young Rachel did for old(er) Rachel was to put some wonderful goals out there to strive for and start a lifetime of learning and trying new things and failing and trying again. And come to think of it, I do have a lava lamp somewhere in the basement, so I guess I am closer to that original vision after all.

For the *Part 1: Looking Back* and *Part 2: Looking Around* tools, I printed my workbook pages and wrote some of the ideas by hand, while other pieces I typed into the worksheets then printed. For the mind map, I prefer to keep it in the hand-written format but there are free mind mapping websites that also work well if you want to convert it to an electronic version at some point. I tend to look through the past and current state worksheets at least once a year, but I don't always make changes.

For the *Part 3: Looking Ahead* tools, I find that keeping my goals and Master Plan in a spreadsheet works best for me. My Master Plan is always changing and would be a mess if I tried to write it all out. Plus, a lot of what is on the plan ends up going right into my Outlook calendar, which sends my phone nice little alerts when something is due, so managing the whole thing from my computer works best for me. Keep in mind if you do go with an app, ensure that it has the capability to print properly formatted 8 ½ by 11-inch pages so that you can print and keep all of your plans together in your Ten Thousand Choices binder.

Here are the data elements I recommend. Feel free to use and make any changes that will help you manage your list.

- Priority
- Element
- Goal
- Choices
- Due Date/Time Frame
- Status
- Success Measure
- Outcome
- Notes

Here is what it looks like in a spreadsheet:

Master Plan Template

Priority (e.g., A1, A2, B1)	Core Element	Goal	Choice(s) Actions, tasks and other activities that you are choosing to do	Due Date When should this be completed? What is the timeframe?	Status (e.g., Not started, In progress, pending, complete, abandoned)	Success Measure(s) What does success look like? How will you know when you have accomplished the goal?	Outcome(s) What happened?	Notes Additional info about goal, progress, changes, constraints, etc.

Step 2: Fill in your work

As with all the assignments, set aside a chunk of quiet time to think about the future you are planning by going through this process. Make sure your completed worksheets are visible. You'll notice that the bulk of your planning is already complete and at your fingertips. You will continue making additions and changes as you go through, but the "heavy lifting" is done.

The first four columns (**Priority, Core Element, Goal** and **Choices**) can be pulled over directly from your Goals to Choices Worksheet. Depending on the choices, you may want to keep them together in one cell or break them out so they each have their own row. My rule is that if the choices each have their own due dates and success measures, they get a row.

Next, review your notes from your completed assignments to fill in the **Due Date, Success Measures** and **Notes** columns. Remember that **Success Measures** tell you when the goal has been completed or choice successfully made. For example, this could be a count of how many phone calls were made to a particular family member during the month. Or it could be the number of hours you spent working out or spending time with your kids or researching your family history. It could be the number of new people you said "hi" to this week or invited to connect on LinkedIn or sent your marketing materials. **Notes** can be used to jot down any other useful information about your goal. You can make a note of changes you made, challenges you have overcome, constraints or issues that you need to address or any other things you need to remember. Depending on how much detail you wrote in your assignments, you may find most of what you need in the mind map, the Goal Prioritization Grid and the Goals and Choices Worksheet.

Finally, you will fill in the **Status** and **Outcome** columns as you work through your goals. Jot down the little wins along the way or final outcome in the **Outcome** column. For example, if your Choice is "Spend eight hours per week working out", you can jot in notes about your average time per week, or a running count for the year, whatever keeps you motivated and on track. It's also a good place to note when you achieved the goal, what happened, how you celebrated, etc.

Optional: You don't have to limit this to the goals and choices from the assignments. If you find it helpful, you can include the other issues, projects and tasks in your life that need resolution on your Master Plan as well. These other activities that make up "the rest of your life" will be competing for time and attention that you give to your goals, so it might be helpful to have them all tracked and accounted for on this table. In addition, it will help you manage the workload of your whole life and all the stress and strain that comes along with having it all floating around in your head. If you use it as such, this document can become the single source for your actions, accomplishments and organization for getting things done. You will be amazed at how relieved you feel and how much more in control of your future you will be when you have everything captured in your Master Plan.

STEP 3: ORGANIZE IT

You can keep your Master Plan neat and organized by using the sort function and by breaking the spreadsheet into sections.

At the end of the table of tasks, draw a thick red line. This is your finish line. Every time you complete an item on the list, you will pick it up and move it below the line. The items at the top then are the ones that are still in play, and the ones below the line are "complete". You can label this divider "Complete" or "Success". Next, draw a thick yellow line about midway down the table. Below this line, place the items that are planned, but not currently underway. You can label this divider "Planned" or "In the Works". Finally add a new thick green line directly under the header. Items below this line are ones you are currently working on. You can label it "Active" or "In Progress".

Master Plan Template

Priority (e.g., A1, A2, B1)	Core Element	Goal	Choice(s) Actions, tasks and other activities that you are choosing to do	Due Date When should this be completed? What is the timeframe?	Status (e.g., Not started, in progress, pending, complete, abandoned)	Success Measure(s) What does success look like? How will you know when you have accomplished the goal?	Outcome What happened?	Notes Additional info about goal, progress, changes, constraints, etc.
Active								
Planned								
Complete								

One thing to keep in mind is that the top "Active" section should never be empty. As you complete items, you will continually be adding new ones from your Planned section. Likewise, as you continually set new goals and actions, you'll add new items to the Planned section. New goals will emerge as your life evolves, new crises will require new actions, and actions you complete may inspire different actions. Use the sorting function (super easy if you are using Excel) to sort by category or priority.

STEP 4: ADD THE FINISHING TOUCHES

Give the whole package a finished look by summing up your vision, elements and top goals on a one-pager that sits on top of the details. This sheet screams "GET STUFF DONE" to you every time you open the book. Go out and buy yourself a fancy three-ring binder to store your plans in. The one-pager will be the first thing you see when you open my binder. Here is Cassie's final summary as an example.

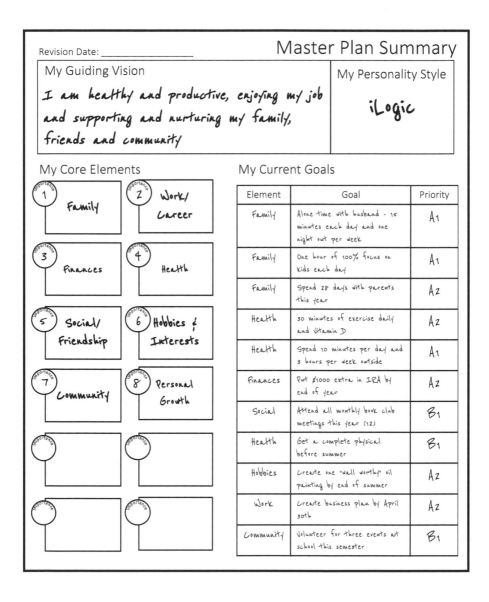

Master Plan Summary

Revision Date: _____

My Guiding Vision

I am healthy and productive, enjoying my job and supporting and nurturing my family, friends and community

My Personality Style

iLogic

My Core Elements

1 Family
2 Work/ Career
3 Finances
4 Health
5 Social/ Friendship
6 Hobbies & Interests
7 Community
8 Personal Growth

My Current Goals

Element	Goal	Priority
Family	Alone time with husband - 15 minutes each day and one night out per week	A1
Family	One hour of 100% focus on kids each day	A1
Family	Spend 28 days with parents this year	A2
Health	30 minutes of exercise daily and Vitamin D	A2
Health	Spend 10 minutes per day and 3 hours per week outside	A1
Finances	Put $1000 extra in IRA by end of year	A2
Social	Attend all monthly book club meetings this year (12)	B1
Health	Get a complete physical before summer	B1
Hobbies	Create one "wall worthy" oil painting by end of summer	A2
Work	Create business plan by April 30th	A2
Community	Volunteer for three events at school this semester	B1

168

The final step in using your Master Plan is to *Use. Your. Master. Plan.* Every single day, use the list to drive your choices. Start with the top items on the list. These are, most importantly, the Active items. You've done all the planning and documenting you can, it's now time to act. Start getting stuff done!

At least weekly, you will need to glance through the Planned items and move anything that's ready to start up to Active. In addition, move anything finished (or canceled) down to the Complete section.

PART THREE TAKEAWAYS:

- Establish a guiding vision that defines the best possible you—that shows you the path ahead and inspires and energizes you to move forward.

- You are more likely to get things done when you set specific and challenging goals versus not setting goals.

- Break your goals down into the choices you will need to make to achieve them.

- Create a Master Plan that ties all of your planning together and drives your choices toward meeting your goals, and your goals toward achieving your vision.

CONCLUSION

CHAPTER FOCUS:

Outcomes | Accountability

ASSIGNMENT:

9. Accountability

All the detailed work is done, now it's time to start working your plan. From my own experience, I know it's hard to keep up the momentum after the flurry of planning is over. No matter how much you want it today, your plan (and your goals with them) could begin to wither and die on the vine after a few months of neglect. From my own experience, I have found roughly three things that account for 99% of the variability in my success at following my plan, and each one is roughly equal in importance.

33%: GET OFF YOUR ARSE.

About a third of what will make this successful is simple brute force —getting up day after day and *making stuff happen*. Make it easy to succeed and hard to fail. Put your plan front and center on your desk. Put reminder notes on your bathroom mirror. Put reminders on your calendar with the most annoying alert sounds you can find. Tell other people what you are doing to put some pressure on yourself to follow through. Whatever it takes to get from zero to step one, then from step one to step two—do it! Break the pattern of inertia or fear or laziness or whatever it is that is keeping you from getting some momentum going.

The most effective way to do it, is to do it.

-Amelia Earhart

33%: WHAT GETS MEASURED GETS DONE.

I just read on the internet (so it must be true) that this saying has been around in some form since the 1500s[13]. There is power in these five words, and the fact that humans are still repeating them after hundreds of years is telling. The things you focus your attention on, especially those that you take the time to observe and measure, are the things that will get the bulk of your time, effort and resources. For each of your goals, you will need to define what success looks like and how you will recognize it when you see it. That is what you are going to measure.

33%: KISS. KEEP. IT. SIMPLE. STUPID.

You've already done the heavy lifting with this planning process. In order for the plan to continue, *it must be easy to maintain going forward.* Your Master Plan is nothing more than the index that references and tracks all of your goals and keeps you focused on the big prize—your guiding vision. We walked through one version of a Master Plan that I've used for years to hold all my moving parts together and remind me what I'm working toward. If it weren't simple, I would have stopped using it long ago.

By the way, I found that the remaining 1% of stuff that may affect your chance of success includes dumb luck, natural disasters, norovirus running rampant in your kid's school and the NHL post-season.

Your Choices

Owning your choices means holding yourself accountable. You can make all the plans and lists you want, but if you don't choose to act on your plan, you will be no further along than when you started this program. Owning your choices is truly where "the rubber meets the road".

ASSIGNMENT 9: OWN YOUR CHOICES

STEP 1: EXECUTE YOUR PLAN

You have done so much excellent work getting to this point, now just follow your own instructions. It's like reading a cookbook.

Every minute spent in planning saves ten minutes in execution.

—*Brian Tracy*

Here are some other tips that may help you get some momentum:

Tell the world. Making a goal public increases your likelihood of success[14]. Announce your intentions, especially for the goals that will involve others. Include them in your planning and keep them abreast of your progress. This will do a couple of good things for you. First, it will give you some social support and cheerleading from your friends and family, which could be the boost you need to get started. Second, it establishes some expectations that you'll get things done. If you keep your plans secret, that makes it too easy to ignore them when things get tough. Out in the open though, you create a little pressure on yourself to act, which is not a bad thing.

Ignore "killer phrases". On the flip side, because many of your goals may require input and cooperation from other people in your life, you'll open yourself up to their opinions. They may enthusiastically support your idea, or they may knowingly or unknowingly shoot it in the heart with a negative response—a "killer phrase". We are bombarded with these negative messages every day, from all directions and sources, including ourselves. Here are some of the classics:

- *Fear and Doubt*: I don't have enough education. I am too old. I am not creative enough. Nobody will support this idea. People will laugh at me behind my back.

- *Excuses*: I don't have time right now. I am not ready yet. It has already been done by someone else. There is too much competition in this space already.

- *Procrastination*: I need to wait and see what happens before I start. Next month will be less hectic. I can always start this tomorrow. I just need to take a break before starting anything else.

- *Nay-Sayers*: It will never work. Why would you want to do that? It will be more trouble than it is worth. Interesting idea, but lots of people have tried it already.

> You really should be focusing on the kids/me right now, not another "project".

When your actions start affecting other people, you must be prepared to overcome resistance. First, be alert for these phrases and identify them as "killer phrases" when you hear them. Jot down some of the killer phrases that you expect to hear from others, and ideas for how you will respond. Second, recognize where they are coming from (people whose opinions matter, or those you can dismiss) and figure out why (e.g., fear, jealousy, legitimate concerns, general curiosity about goal). Third, assuming you've done your legwork on your plan, be ready to defend it, answer questions and convince them it will work.

Measure your progress. It is worth repeating—"what gets measured gets done". If you don't have clear measures for your goals and you haven't written down how the outcomes will be measured, go back and do that now. Seriously. You're shooting yourself in the foot if you don't. Gauging your progress will create a positive feedback loop that pushes you along and will also give you a poke in the forehead if you're falling behind. Do it.

Reward yourself. As you measure your progress, you will be keeping a running tab on your accomplishments. Celebrate them! You absolutely deserve and need to give yourself credit for making good choices and for achieving your goals. As long as your celebrating doesn't wreck other goals you set, you should splurge on those new boots or help yourself to the cookies as a reward for all your hard work. Acknowledging your success doesn't have to be a splurge either, it could simply be that—acknowledging to yourself that you have made progress. Smile. Give yourself a hug.

Forgive yourself. Going through this process should make you feel better, not worse. I didn't do my job if you are using this plan to beat up on yourself for not accomplishing everything you set out to do. Making mistakes, missing deadlines, not reaching goals—these are a fundamental part of being human. When something doesn't go quite like you planned, take some time to analyze what happened, accept the lesson learned, forgive yourself and move on.

Strive for progress, not perfection.

Know that execution is not a one-time event, it is a continuous effort. The good news is that the more you get done and the more positive changes you see in your life, the more "getting things done" will become a habit. Each success creates more momentum to keep pushing forward, which over time becomes a veritable avalanche of good things happening in your life.

This is a commitment—follow through on it just like any other promise you might make. Hopefully you keep your promises. If not, then you should add that to your goals. If you do keep promises and would never dream of letting down a friend or loved one, give yourself the same respect. You are making a vow to yourself to create the life you desire—follow through on that commitment!

STEP 2: GIVE YOURSELF A MID-YEAR REVIEW

Owning your choices boils down to relentlessly executing, measuring, tracking and reviewing the things you've accomplished, the actions taken and the goals you've met. I recommend a year-round planning cycle that has three formal "planning and review sessions" that are scheduled on the calendar. The first session is the New Year planning session. You can do this at any time throughout the year, but it is easy to be inspired by the fresh start a new year promises, so consider doing your first planning session in early January. Next, schedule two formal review sessions throughout the year, to take some time and think about progress on the goals set in January, if anything needs to change about the goals, or to add new goals. The first should happen at the mid-point of the year, so if you are beginning your year in January, this would be sometime during the summer. The second review session is the "final review" to see performance versus goals over the course of the year. Complete this sometime in December so you are fresh and ready to start again in January. However, you schedule your planning and review cycle, the important things are to A.) *Value yourself* enough to set aside the time to do it, and B.) put it on your calendar so you don't forget.

For the mid-year review in the summer, I recommend a glass of sweet tea or lemonade or sangria and some summer mood music. Get out your updated copy of your goal sheet and a red Sharpie. I like the grade-school method of evaluation, that is, a simple letter grade. You can use any method you like; my advice is just keep it simple and don't make yourself cry. If the memory of a sadistic Third Grade teacher's red pen comes flooding back, forget the letter grade and just give yourself checkmarks or something. I use the A, B, C, D and F grading system, and sometimes add in the plusses and minuses for extra differentiation if needed.

Your review sessions will use the tools you've already been using in the planning process. You'll just add progress notes and put the finishing touches on them during the sessions. We have a couple of tools to review and revise your plans. The first is one you've already created, the Master Plan. The second tool you will use during your mid-year and final review sessions is the Goals to Choices Worksheet. You will see two new columns added to the sheet (see example) to evaluate your performance on the various goals. You can also use these columns to make notes or adjustments based on how the situation or the goal itself changed.

Goals to Choices Worksheet

Priority	Core Element	Goal	Choices	Mid Year Review	Year End Review
A₂	Family	To keep us strongly connected, the kids, my parents and I will spend at least 28 days together during this year	• Spend two weeks with them this summer • Force them to do video calls with kids • Invite them to visit in the fall • Call 3x per week during day (short chats)	B	
A₁	Family	Of the "free time" we have between school and bed time each day, one hour of that should be focused 100% on the kids	• Weekly family game night (Monday) • Eat dinner together as a family every weeknight • Screens/devices away during devoted time • Have one favorite show we watch together	A	
B₁	Family	To keep us connected with my extended family, we should "see" each other at least 12 times this year	• Plan one visit every 2 months • Video call with all the kids weekly • Put kids in charge of birthday cards	C	
A₁	Family	To keep relationship strong, we need to spend at least 15 minutes alone each day and do something together alone once per week	• Date night with husband once per month, no kids • Walk the dog with husband alone every evening • Do treadmill while he is working out	B	

So, going back to the goals Cassie set for her Family Core Element, she took a minute to consider each goal and the choices that were supposed to get her closer to that goal. Since it was mid-year, she thought about how well she was doing on those actions as of the first six months only (not taking into account what is planned, remember this is your actual performance as of your mid-year review date). For the first goal, she wanted to spend more time with her parents, and put a target of twenty-eight days out there. As of mid-year, she was not thrilled with her progress. She had planned a trip, but hadn't completed the two weeks yet, so couldn't give herself full credit for that. She had done a couple of video calls but hadn't been able to get into a weekly habit, so that was okay, but not great. She did remember to mention a fall trip to her parents, and they were mulling it over, so she gave herself credit for that. All in all, by mid-year she felt this goal was at a "B" grade. This was by no means a failure of her planning, it is simply information that she used to motivate herself and put more effort and resources into a top goal.

Her second goal, to spend more quality time with her kids, was also prioritized highly and linked directly to her vision (to support and nurture her family). The two actions she planned were going very well—they implemented a weekly family game night on Mondays, which they almost always managed to do. Every Monday evening, Cassie had to *make a choice* in order to ensure this happened. She had to *choose* to put down her book or close her laptop and rally the family for the games. She had to *choose* to pull the kids away from their screens even though she knew they would whine. She had to *choose* to turn off the TV in spite of husbandly grumbles. Sometimes she didn't feel like playing games or cajoling the family to participate. Sometimes they had to shift the night around due to sports and other activities. *But the fact that she set this is a high-priority goal that supported her vision and tracked it weekly kept it in the front of her mind and gave her the extra motivation to see it through.* She definitely felt this one was a success.

The other choice for this goal was also going swimmingly, as they all made a concentrated effort to eat together at the dinner table instead of in front of the TV or at separate times as they got finished with homework, playing outside or yardwork. Just like all of her goals, this one was achieved by *making the conscious choice* over and over to eat together. This included choosing to do all the preparation, communication, coaxing and work that made it happen. To turn off the television, to put away the snacks, to yell up the stairs multiple times and to ask her daughter to set the table and her son to help with the drinks and then firmly ask the family to sit down at the table and not start eating until everyone was there. The choice itself was easier because of the plan, but the effort was still required to make it happen. Some days were easier than others, but because it was an important goal to Cassie, and one that directly tied to her vision, she chose to put in the effort. By mid-year, this goal got an "A". Cassie was proud of her progress but didn't want to lose momentum just because the first part of the year had gone so well.

STEP 3: CONDUCT A YEAR-END REVIEW AND START THE PROCESS OVER

In December, after working her plan another six months, Cassie repeated the review process. Starting with her first top-priority goal for the year in the Family Element, Cassie evaluated spending more time with her parents. Again, she put down a target of twenty-eight days. By December, she had not only spent the two weeks with her parents, but they also came to visit in the fall for ten days. Those in-person visits combined with the weekly Facetime calls, which they finally got into a good habit of doing, got Cassie to her goal and beyond. She felt this goal was met with stunning success and gave herself an A+.

Goals to Choices Worksheet

Priority	Core Element	Goal	Choices	Mid Year Review	Year End Review
A2	Family	To keep us strongly connected, the kids, my parents and I will spend at least 28 days together during this year	• Spend two weeks with them this summer • Force them to do video calls with kids • Invite them to visit in the fall • Call 3x per week during day (short chats)	B	A+
A1	Family	Of the "free time" we have between school and bed time each day, one hour of that should be focused 100% on the kids	• Weekly family game night (Monday) • Eat dinner together as a family every weeknight • Screens/devices away during devoted time • Have one favorite show we watch together	A	A
B1	Family	To keep us connected with my extended family, we should "see" each other at least 12 times this year	• Plan one visit every 2 months • Video call with all the kids weekly • Put kids in charge of birthday cards	C	D
A1	Family	To keep relationship strong, we need to spend at least 15 minutes alone each day and do something together alone once per week	• Date night with husband once per month, no kids • Walk the dog with husband alone every evening • Do treadmill while he is working out	B	B-

The second goal, and again one that was high priority, was to spend more quality time with her kids. The two actions planned for this goal had been going quite well as of July. However, their progress slowed as the fall progressed, and then went off the rails during the holidays. They were only able to eat dinner together occasionally during the last few months of the year due to sports (a conflicting choice) and had abandoned family game night altogether (in hindsight, Cassie regretted not making the tough choices that would have kept game night going). She might have given this goal a lower rating, but in addition to the planned choices, they chose to do other things that contributed to the goal of spending more quality time together. During the fall, they went on a trip to Shenandoah National Park to see the gorgeous fall foliage, and during the holidays they spent quality time together wrapping gifts, decorating the house and making cookies. So even though the planned actions didn't work out as well as she had hoped, the goal itself was fresh in her mind and driving her to make different choices that were aligned with the vision of supporting and nurturing her family, so Cassie gave herself another A on that one.

The next goal on the example was not a top priority, but it's worth noting. This happens from time to time, you have the best of intentions, you set a worthy goal and make some plans to meet it, but then just cannot make it happen. Preferably this happens to be one of the lower-priority goals, or one that you can still try for in the future (not one where the opportunity is gone). For Cassie, this goal was one of those. She wants to keep her family connected with her husband's family. That is why she set a goal, and then put in place what she thought were some simple choices to make it happen. It turned out to be more difficult than she expected. By mid-year, she managed to get to visit once, and thanks to several spring birthdays, a handful of video calls. In July that earned a C, but she hoped for better performance in the fall. Unfortunately, this goal fell off the rails after that. During the last six months of the year, they made a couple of calls and because of everyone's work and travel schedules, they were not able to arrange a visit. They managed to spend two weekends together over the course of an entire year.

What do you do in this case? Well, first you learn from it. Spend some time reflecting on what happened, ask yourself:

- Why did I set this goal in the first place?
- Did my priorities change over the year?
- What got in the way of meeting this goal?
- Were the choices not appropriate for the goal?
- Did I lack the time, resources, or motivation to achieve the goal?
- Were there external factors that became barriers to achieving the goal? What could have been done to clear those barriers?
- Do I have enough control over this situation for this to be a realistic goal?

Second, you decide whether this is a goal you want to carry forward in your Master Plan or not. It may be a worthy goal, but you may find that after having an honest conversation with yourself, it is not one you will ever put the time and resources toward. At that point, you can either just not include it in the next year's plan, or you can downgrade the priority, so it's there as a reminder, or "nice to have", but won't supersede any of the higher priority goals going forward.

This is not an indication that your plan isn't working. Just the opposite! Your plan is meant to adapt to reality and evolve as your life changes. You are laying out what you want to do at a single point in time, but life keeps coming at you and doesn't always bend to your will. Your plan is helping you bob and weave and work your way toward your larger vision, but no plan is perfect. Events in your life can change your goals over time. A "C" or an "F" isn't failure, it's simply information for you to use either to reassess your actions or to reprioritize your goals and try again!

FINAL THOUGHTS ABOUT THE PLANNING PROCESS

This planning process and the Master Plan are *not* the ends in themselves, they are your vehicle for driving forward and making good choices. You aren't just hopping in and taking off for parts unknown, you now have a clear vision of your destination and a map for getting there quickly and safely, and just to squeeze a little more out of this metaphor, a "dashboard" of success measures you can build on for future journeys!

In preparing for battle, I have always found that plans are useless, but planning is indispensable.
—*Dwight D. Eisenhower*

I have seen this quote from Dwight D. Eisenhower about planning, but it took me a long time to understand what he meant. It was while driving my car that it dawned on me. I was going somewhere I hadn't been before, taking wrong turns, and the GPS kept saying the word "recalculating". I was laughing that "she" (the GPS voice lady, we named her Mappy) was probably getting really tired of continually having to scrap her plan and come up with a new route for getting me to my destination.

This is exactly what President Ike meant when he said plans are useless. As soon as you miss the first turn, the static plan in the GPS is no longer valid. You can't make any more turns based on that plan, because you missed the first turn. Hence all the "recalculating". The act of planning is just like that. It forces you to think clearly about your destination and focus your brain on how to get there. Sure, turns may be missed, and mistakes may be made. That is human nature. But because you've gone through the act of planning, you can easily readjust your planned actions to get back on track. Missteps will happen again and again, but you'll continue to plan and readjust and in doing this eventually achieve your goals.

Well, that's it my friend. You are ready to work the heck out of this plan. You've realized by now that this planning process never ends. Of course, you make your good choices and achieve goals along the way, and take the time to celebrate those successes, but you'll always add new goals and make choices to push yourself closer and closer to your guiding vision. The results are a never-ending chain of small and large successes that keep you "unstuck" and moving forward, continually creating the life you want and focused on your true purpose.

In the long run, we shape our lives, and we shape ourselves. The process never ends until we die. And the choices we make are ultimately our own responsibility.

-Eleanor Roosevelt

FINAL TAKEAWAYS:

- Get moving! The planning is finished, it is time to act.
- Define what success looks like and measure your progress.
- Take accountability for your actions (or inactions).
- Learn from your mistakes, then forgive yourself and move on!

Acknowledgments

I am so very grateful for all the help I received:

First and foremost, Ed, for your encouragement and support. You do such a good job of listening to my rants then guiding me back to reality.

Paul Gillard, Amy Damoulakis, Nick Damoulakis, Rachele Lowery and Aaron Sigler for slogging through early versions of this book and providing both critical feedback and reassurance when I needed it most.

Katie Silver, Monica Robyns, Hillary Broder, Jill Gillard, Stacey Donaldson, Amy Pontius and Emily Grimshaw, who generously shared their stories and experiences.

Polgarus Studio, Lee Thompson and Judy Lyne, for editing and proofreading support; and Julie Hopkins, for cover design.

All the colleagues, friends and family who listened to me moan and groan, then encouraged me (nicely, but rightly so) to shut up and follow my own advice. From my heart, thank you for your feedback, suggestions and help working through ideas and challenges.

Appendix 1: Ten Thousand Choices Binder Contents

Front Cover: **Master Plan** **Summary**	•Completed Master Plan Summary sheet for current year
Tab 1: **My Current Year**	•20XX Master Plan •Mind Map and notes •Goal Prioritization Grid •Goals to Choices Worksheets •Goal Statement Worksheets •Mid　Year Review •Year—End Review
Tab 2: **My Life**	•Personal Style Quiz and best-fit profile •Notable Choices and Lessons Learned Worksheets •Current version of Personal Summary Worksheet •Core Elements Worksheet, Mind Map Template and notes •Guiding Vision
Tab 3: **My Archive**	•Archived versions of planning documents •Completed projects

Tab 4: My Resources	•Articles, blog posts, interesting reads •Notes

Appendix 2: Assignment Summary

PART 1: LOOK BACK

- Assignment 1: Identify your personal style
  - Step 1: Complete the personal style quiz
  - Step 2: Explore your personal style profile
- Assignment 2: Understand your past choices
  - Step 1: Think about your past
  - Step 2: Identify notable choices
  - Step 3: Reflect on lessons learned

PART 2: LOOK AROUND

- Assignment 3: Write your personal summary
- Assignment 4: Identify your core elements
  - Step 1: Brainstorm
  - Step 2: Sort your ideas into common themes
  - Step 3: Define each core element
- Assignment 5: Prioritize your core elements

PART 3: LOOK AHEAD

- Assignment 6: Define your guiding vision
  - Step 1: Visualize your future self
  - Step 2: Write down the key ideas
  - Step 3: Create your vision statement
- Assignment 7: Set your goals and plan your choices

- o Step 1: Brainstorm potential goals
  - o Step 2: Prioritize your raw goals
  - o Step 3: Write clear goal statements
  - o Step 4: Turn your goals into CHOICES
- Assignment 8: Write your Master Plan
  - o Step 1: Pick your tool
  - o Step 2: Fill in your work
  - o Step 3: Organize it
  - o Step 4: Add the finishing touches

CONCLUSION

- Assignment 9: Own your choices
  - o Step 1: Execute your plan
  - o Step 2: Give yourself a mid-year review
  - o Step 3: Conduct a year-end review and start the process over

  - o

Appendix 3: Recommended Reading

PSYCHOLOGY AND PERSONAL STYLE

Hogan, Robert T., *Personality: Theories and Applications*. Tulsa, OK: Hogan Press, 2008.

Keirsey, David, *Please Understand Me II: Temperament, Character, Intelligence*. Del Mar, CA: Prometheus Nemesis Book Company, 1998.

Miscisin, Mary, *Showing Our True Colors*. True Colors, Publisher, 2001.

Myers, Isabel Briggs. Revised by Linda K. Kirby and Katharine D. Myers. *Introduction to Type, 5ᵗʰ Edition* Consulting Psychologists Press, Inc., 1993.

DECISION MAKING, GOAL SETTING AND OTHER GOOD STUFF

Aros, Claudio, *The Magic of Mental Diagrams: Expand your Memory, Enhance your Concentration and Learn to Apply Logic*. Skyhorse Publishing, 2006.

Edwards, Betty, *Drawing on the Right Side of the Brain, Revised Edition*. New York: Tarcher, 1989.

Hammond, J. S., Keeney, R. L., & Raiffa, H., *Smart Choices: A Practical Guide to Making Better Life Decisions*. Boston: Harvard Business School Press, 1999.

Iyengar, Sheena, *The Art of Choosing*. New York: Twelve, 2010.

Locke, E. A. "Motivation Through Conscious Goal Setting." *Applied and Preventative Psychology* 5 (1996): 117-124.

Nunbert, Geoff (2018). "So Longhand: Has Cursive Reached the End of the Line?" *Fresh Air*. Read by Geoff Numberg, May 31, 2018. Accessed May 31, 2018. https://www.npr.org/2018/05/31/612197167/so-longhand-has-cursive-reached-the-end-of-the-line.

Pande, Peter, Neuman, Robert. P. and Cavanagh, Roland R., *The Six Sigma Way Team Fieldbook: An Implementation Guide for Process Improvement Teams*. New York: McGraw Hill, 2002.

Vedantam, Shankar, "Check Yourself", *Hidden Brain* (podcast), October 30, 2017, accessed January 1, 2018, https://www.npr.org/2017/10/30/559996276/the-trick-to-surviving-a-high-stakes-high-pressure-job-try-a-checklist .

About the Author

Rachel Radwinsky, PhD is an industrial/organizational psychologist, author and personal effectiveness coach who helps people improve a core driver of their lives – their choices. She commandeers the most valuable self-improvement tools and techniques from the disciplines of psychology, business, quality and technology makes them accessible to all.

She is founder of MCT Associates, LLC, a practice focused on helping people and organizations master their choices by envisioning their ideal futures and creating and executing the plans for achieving them. Her coaching system is based on the Ten Thousand Choices program and a coach training curriculum is also available to eligible practitioners.

Dr. Radwinsky lives in Frederick, Maryland with her husband, kids and awesome dog.

Message from the Author

Dear You,

Thanks for hanging in there. I feel like I know you. Perhaps we have some things in common. I am somewhere in "mid-life". I went to school, got married, got a job, and had kids. I have had a few different jobs; some were good, some were atrocious. I've moved around a little. Have had a couple of little health issues here and there. I haven't experienced a divorce, but I was just lucky to have found a good partner the first time around. I've lost people I have loved – both to death and to distance. Let's see, what else? I've been to Disney. I have a really good dog (I mean REALLY GOOD, best boy ever) and a family and group of friends I am quite fond of.

Your story may be different. Maybe you didn't go to Disney. Maybe you have a cat. Maybe you are still looking for your soul mate. But I'll bet it's not too far off.

I know sometimes it feels like we are the only ones in the universe with our particular set of challenges, but by and large, our lives follow the same pattern. We are born, we do things, we die (my daughter would call that a Debbie Downer statement). The differences we think we see between us and others are really not that large. In general, we are all just trying make the most of those "things" in the middle, between birth and death. We all just have different ways of going about that.

So, I'll say it again, life is short. I am serious about milking this life of every single drop of goodness, enjoyment, love, meaning and value that I possibly can. The only way to do that is to make sure that my choices lead me there, to that value, to that good. Every choice that takes me away from the good wastes my priceless time and diminishes the joy that I want to experience in this short little blip of time called my life.

So, fellow human just making your way in the world, thanks for reading my book. I hope it helps you get control over your choices and improve your life. I would love to hear from you. Go to my website and sign up for my blog updates or download free worksheets and sample plans. Join my Facebook group to connect with others working through similar challenges. Shoot me an email and let me know how your plans are coming along or share some of your own planning experiences and advice, or just say hi.

Email: rachel@tenthousandchoices.com
Facebook Page: @TenThousandChoices
Facebook Group: Ten Thousand Choices
Website: www.tenthousandchoices.com

Notes

[1] May, Cindy. "A Learning Secret: Don't Take Notes with a Laptop." *Scientific American*, June 3, 2014.

[2] "Schadenfreude." Wikipedia, Wikimedia Foundation, 29 May 2018, en.wikipedia.org/wiki/Schadenfreude.

[3] www.siop.org

[4] Locke, E. A., Shaw, K. N., Saari, L. M., & Latham, G. P. "Goal Setting and TaskPerformance: 1969–1980." *Psychological Bulletin*, 90(1) (1981): 125-152.

[5] Glasser, William. *Choice Theory: A New Psychology of Personal Freedom.* New York: Harper, 1998.

[6] Einhorn, H. J. and Hogarth, R. M. "Behavioral Decision Theory: Processes of Judgement and Choices." *Annual Review of Psychology*, 32(1) 1981: 53-88.

[7] Hogan, Robert T. *Personality: Theories and Applications.* Tulsa, OK: Hogan Press, 2008.

[8] Keirsey, David. *Please Understand Me II: Temperament, Character, Intelligence.* Del Mar, CA: Prometheus Nemesis Book Company, 1998.

[9] Jung, Carl. G. *Psychological Types.* New York: Harcourt, Brace and Company, 1923.

[10] "Butterfly effect." Wikipedia, Wikimedia Foundation, 7 Dec. 2017, en.wikipedia.org/wiki/Butterfly_effect. For a more detailed explanation, I suggest Gleik, J. (2008). *Chaos: Making a New Science.* New York: Penguin. For a fun short story that

---

illustrates the concept, I recommend "The Sound of Thunder" by Ray Bradbury.

[11] Pande, P. S., Neuman, R. P., and Cavanagh, R. R. *The Six Sigma Way Team Fieldbook*. New York: McGraw-Hill, 2002.

[12] Locke, E. A., and G. P. Latham. *Goal Setting: A Motivational Technique that Works*. Englewood Cliffs, NJ: Prentice Hall, 1984.

[13] Discussion of the origin of the quote "What gets measured gets done" http://www.matthewcornell.org/blog/2007/7/30/whats-your-feed-reading-speed.html#1

[14] Hollenbeck, J. R., Williams, C. R., & Klein, H. J. "An Empirical Examination of the Antecedents of Commitment to Difficult Goals." *Journal of Applied Psychology*, 74(1), 1989: 18-23.

Made in the USA
Lexington, KY
12 July 2018